ROBERTA HORTON

SCRAP·QUILTS of

the art of making do

C&T PUBLISHING

Scrap Quilts: The Art of Making Do
©1998 Roberta Horton
Illustrations©1998 C&T Publishing, Inc.

Editor: Liz Aneloski
Technical Editor: Sara Kate MacFarland
Copy Editor: Judith Moretz
Cover & Book Designer: Micaela Miranda Carr
Design Director: Diane Pedersen
Illustrators: Lina Liu, Jay Richards, Jill Berry and Lisa Kreishok
Photographer: Sharon Risedorph, unless otherwise noted
Published by C&T Publishing, Inc., P.O. Box 1456, Lafayette, California 94549

Children's sewing machines pictured throughout are from the collection of the author.
Front cover quilt *Ode to my Featherweight*, Roberta Horton. Back cover quilt *Three Birds, Two Fish & a Pot of Flowers*, Nancy Freeman.

Library of Congress Cataloging-in-Publication Data
Horton, Roberta.
      Scrap quilts : the art of making do / Roberta Horton.
           p. cm.
      Includes bibliographical references and index.
      ISBN 1-57120-047-9
      1. Patchwork--Patterns. 2. Quilting--Patterns. 3. Patchwork quilts. I. Title
TT835.H627   1998
746.46--dc21   98-14465
                                  CIP

Printed in the United States

10   9   8   7   6   5   4   3   2   1

TABLE OF CONTENTS

DEDICATION

This book is written for
all those individuals who
have said to me,

**"I can't
do that,
I'm a
traditional
quiltmaker."**

There is a dual focus to this book: fabric and scrap quilts. I can't separate the two. In this day and age, many quiltmakers seem interested only in how fast they can make a quilt. I'm more concerned about how well my fabric is showcased within my quilts. Complicated patterns don't turn me on when I make a quilt—each time, it's the fabric that's the most important factor.

FOREWORD

Antique scrap quilts can be the most humble of quilts and, at the same time, the most complicated of all quilts to understand. I consider them to be the truest reflection of America's past because they are what the average quiltmaker made. Scrap quilts were made by the masses, not the wealthy elite. I'm referring to the quiltmaker who lived in a log cabin, a sod house, a farmhouse, or a bungalow, and not to the woman who lived in a mansion. Scrap quilts were made to be used. They were unpretentious and honest—and, at the same time, beautiful.

This book is divided into six chapters. First, I have given you my definition and explanation of what I consider to be a scrap quilt. This took me years to understand. Then there is a large section on fabric and how to understand its use in a scrap quilt.

Next, there are case studies of pieced scrap quilts and quilts that combine piecing and appliqué. I have included a folk art section to encourage creativity. Finally, there is a chapter on how to accomplish the technical aspects of making an actual quilt. This isn't about sewing a quarter-inch seam. It's the information I feel will allow you to go beyond where you are now. How to create your own patterns, whether they be pieced or appliquéd. How to cut directly into the fabric as opposed to relying on a rigid master plan to make your quilt.

So, sit back and enjoy *Scrap Quilts: The Art of Making Do*. Savor the old and new scrap quilts I have collected for your perusal. Keep your mind open to the ideas I have presented and really look with your eyes at the many examples. Do try the exercises I have suggested in the skills chapter—they really work. I hope this book will give you many ideas for your next quilt.

This hand-crank children's sewing machine started me down a wonderful path of continuous, never-ending stitches.

What does it mean to be a traditional quiltmaker? Usually, it alludes to the fact that the individual is used to working in established pathways, often using patterns created by someone else. In the area of piecing, the pattern is one that has been around for awhile—sometimes for over a hundred years. For quilters who work in an appliqué format, the motif frequently comes from a pattern book or a commercially-produced pattern kit. My job is to show you how you can make these time-honored and/or borrowed patterns your own.

The most recent individual who proclaimed her traditional stance to me (referred to in the dedication on page 4) then proceeded to create her own original composition entitled *Prairie Flowers* (page 7) in a Folk Art Quilts workshop. Edna Mowchenko later said, "I enjoyed making this quilt right down to the last stitch. For the first time I've made something that wasn't planned ahead. I've learned to be creative, and this won't be the last folk art quilt I make."

I'm convinced that hiding inside all of us is a creative side which we don't always access. Sometimes we don't even realize it exists. Being creative merely means that we make our own choices, and we learn to be satisfied with our own images or our own version of how a quilt should or can be made.

This book is filled with photographs of both antique and newly-made quilts. The old quilts are included as inspiration for coloration and fabric usage. From these wonderful quilts we can deduce guidelines and rules to follow. As we learn to understand fabric pattern and color better, we can become more creative and confident in our own selections for our quilts.

INTRODUCTION

Some antique quilts were also selected for their composition choices. For some reason, a disproportionate number feature unique solutions to problems encountered along the way.

Several quilts are finished with only two borders; another is only three and a half rows wide. Upon close scrutiny, one quilt top features a change of pattern within the perimeter blocks. That's my eye searching for the unusual solution.

Because these are traditional quilts, I have an answer for all the individuals who have innocently told me they couldn't do something because they were traditional quiltmakers. Learn to see with your eyes what the tradition really is. These antique quilts serve as a validation of the possibilities and options. Strive to keep your mind and eyes open.

The quilters who made these old quilts were creative. It's easy for us to recognize that quality in someone else's work, especially if there is also the added stamp of approval of age. How, then, can we inject the magic ingredient of creativity into our own work? Let me share with you the recipe . . . .

Prairie Flowers 43" x 44". 1997. Edna Mowchenko, Moose Jaw, Saskatchewan, Canada.

SCRAP QUILTS 1

WHAT IS A SCRAP QUILT?

What a riddle! It has taken me years of study to come up with the answers. There is indeed a formula, or at least there's a list of possible ingredients. Let's take each part separately so you, too, can have the answers.

The Delectable Mountains
66" x 78". 1991. Becky Goldsmith, Sherman, Texas. Does this look like a scrap quilt to you? The judges ruled no! (Block pattern page 136)

As a new quiltmaker in the early seventies, I eagerly began buying antique pieced quilts. As I inventory my collection, I realize that I mainly purchased scrap quilts. Somehow I've always been drawn to them. Why? Perhaps in the beginning it was because I didn't understand them; that is, I didn't know how to make one myself. That was the mystery, the drawing power, of a scrap quilt.

HERE ARE THE PIECES OF THE PUZZLE AND THE APPROPRIATE ANSWERS:

1. How many fabrics should be in a scrap quilt?

Is there a magic number that qualifies a quilt to be called a scrap quilt? I don't think so, but I heard a story of a quilt moved out of the scrap category in a national competition because it contained only sixty-five rather than their required seventy-five fabrics.

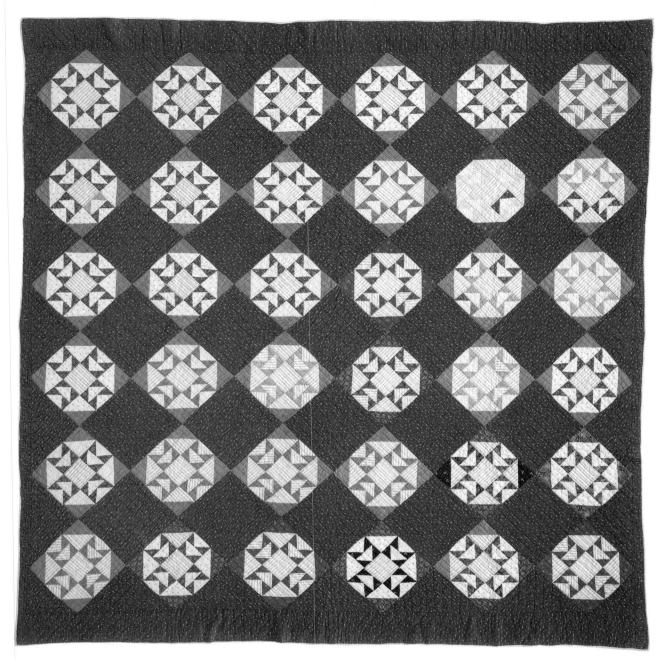

Capital T
86" x 85". Circa 1910. Collection of author.

I got out my scrap quilts, or I should say, the ones *I* consider to be scrap quilts. Some were indeed "legal," but others lacked the requisite seventy-five fabrics. For goodness sakes, my *Capital T* had only eleven fabrics! Yet it still felt like a scrap quilt to me. There must be some other factors to consider if a quilt is to be classified as a scrap quilt.

2. **Why does the use of a lot of fabrics make a quilt more interesting?**

I love fabric, so quilts made with a lot of different fabrics give me more to look at, more to love. I am forced to read the entire surface of the quilt to find all the variety in the fabric patterns and colors. It's sort of like a treasure hunt. In contrast, I only have to read one of the blocks in a repeat-block quilt if the fabric usage is

duplicated. It doesn't seem to matter how complicated and complex the construction of an individual block may be. Once is enough! That quilt-maker wasted a lot of effort to entertain me; there's nothing new for me to see. A pillow or cushion would have consumed as much of my interest and curiosity.

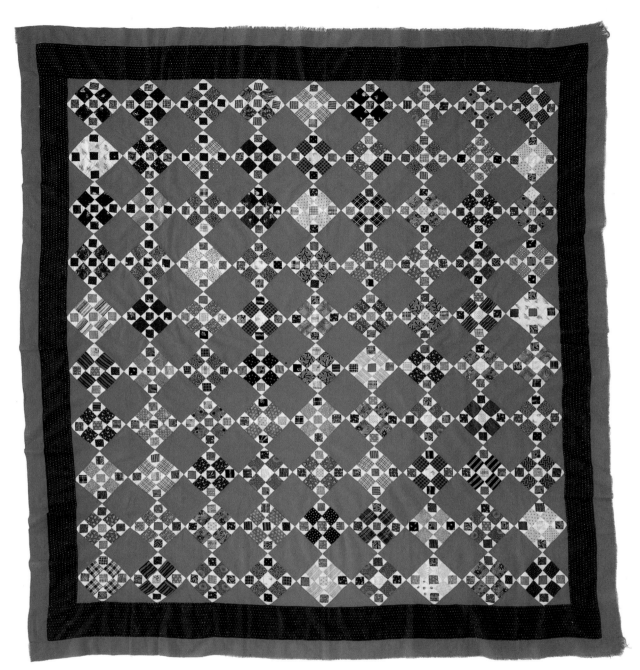

Ninepatch (top)
70" x 80". 1880-90s. Collection of author. Blocks are set on point alternately with squares of plain turkey red.

Here's another thought. A scrap quilt is impossible to memorize. It would require a lengthy phone conversation to a fellow quiltmaker to describe a good scrap quilt. Not so for the repeat-fabric quilt. All that would be necessary would be a short statement which includes the pattern, the block size, and a brief inventory of the fabrics.

Ninepatch is constructed from a fairly simple pattern. Plain red alternate blocks separate the ninepatches. The two-strip border of blue and red nicely frames the composition. If all the blocks duplicated the fabric used in the first block in the first row it wouldn't require much effort to look at it. It would be strong and graphic, but a short phone conversation.

3. Why are some fabrics in an antique scrap quilt ugly?

Ofttimes I've admired a scrap quilt only to discover that I didn't like some of the fabrics used in it. I probably wouldn't have bought that fabric in the first place. At least, I wouldn't have had certain fabrics touch each other in a shared seam. How could this be?

Detail of *Turning A New Leaf*. For full quilt see page 71.

It's important to understand the relationships between fabrics. They don't all do the same job within a quilt or a block. Some are there to catch our attention, others merely cover the batting. Some form a contrast so we can better appreciate the beauty of another one.

Study the detail showing four neighboring blocks in *Turning A New Leaf*. Would you have combined these particular fabrics within each block? Would you have had these specific blocks touch each other? It's difficult to imagine how Debby Altfeld selected these four sets of fabrics to reside next to each other. Yet when you view the whole quilt on page 71 you will see that the result is wonderful. The understanding of fabric is so important that I have devoted a whole separate chapter to the subject.

4. Scrap quilts often appear to contain more than one block pattern when in reality they can be built using the same block pattern throughout. How is this accomplished?

First of all, I was born an appliquér, which means I had to learn to visualize in the geometry of piecing. Initially, I thought the antique repeat block pieced quilts were composed of many different patterns. I now know the pattern templates used in each block were identical but the placement of value (the degree of lightness or darkness) within the block was inconsistent. This results in a variation of the perceived images.

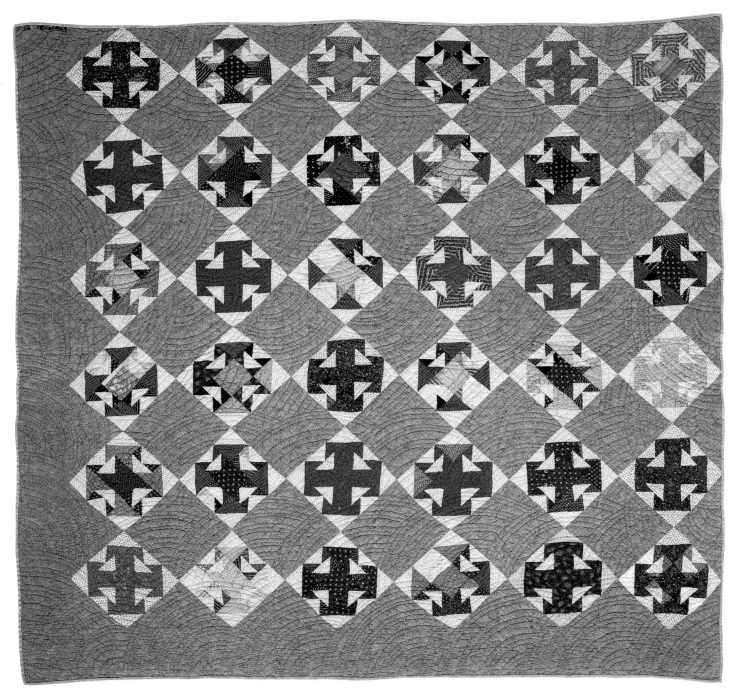

Scrap Double T
77" x 76". Circa 1880. Collection of Helen Temple Cummins, Carmichael, California. (Block pattern page 137). Notice that there are borders on only two sides of the quilt

Look at *Scrap Double T* Block #1, Row #1 (upper left hand block in the quilt) as the role model. Block #2, Row #1 (the block to the right) showcases a square on point in the center. In Block #3, Row #1 you're more aware of the dark red triangles. Do you notice how your eye keeps searching for the variations?

Mariner's Compass
70" x 92". Circa 1870. Collection of Nancyann J. Twelker, Shoreline, Washington.
This quilt features borders on only two sides of the quilt.

Mariner's Compass features some blocks in which the fabric use, and therefore the value use, is identical. Find them. (One combination appears four times; another appears twice.) It's permissible to clone some of the blocks in a scrap quilt. You will notice that the two sets read differently from each other (compare Block #1, Row #4 and Block #3, Row #4). Sharper contrasts between these two variations can be seen if you compare Block #1, Row #1 to Block #2, Row #2.

5. I would think a scrap quilt seen in its entirety was beautiful, only to discover that the look of some of the individual blocks was downright ugly. The composition of one block wouldn't look good as a pillow. This seems to be a contradiction. How does it work?

Varying the value within blocks gives you variations so the viewer isn't bored. Some of the variations are pleasing to look at, while others appear awkward or cumbersome if viewed singly. The awkward block once again provides contrast. It allows us to better appreciate the beautifully balanced or proportional block.

6. Blocks often appear to be of different sizes within a scrap quilt. How can you make this happen?

When a scrap quilt is displayed on a wall, some of the blocks can look bigger than others. I now know that light fabrics are seen as larger. Likewise, the substitution of a darker fabric can make that same area look smaller. For example, if you vary the value of the background fabrics used in your blocks, they may magically appear to be of different sizes. Look at *Square On A Square* on page 26. Block #2, Row #4 has the lightest background and therefore appears to be the largest block in the quilt.

If the fabric used in the perimeter background shapes of a block is in value contrast to the unit next to it, you will see the outline of the block more clearly, as in the block just mentioned. If instead, the perimeter background area blends in with the next area (plain alternate block, sashing, or another block), then only part of the image shows. Look again at *Square On A Square* on page 26. Block #5, Row #5 and Block #3, Row #7 read as miniature blocks within the quilt.

Or, look at *Ninepatch* on page 11, which features some blocks that read as larger than their companions. When a lighter fabric has been used for the four squares within the block, the whole block reads lighter, and therefore larger.

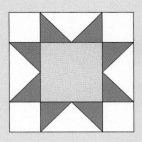

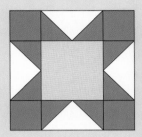

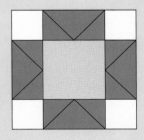

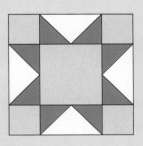

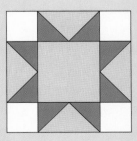

Eight Pointed Star block variations show how value placement can change the appearance of a block

7. Some of the blocks don't show clearly. That is, they seem to disappear. Is this okay? Can it even be desirable?

I call these wonderful units "fade-out blocks." Sometimes a particular fabric has naturally aged or lost its color faster than its mates. Value contrasts that initially existed have disappeared. Or, the quiltmaker may have thought it was sufficient to put different colors together in a block, but not different values.

Capital T on page 10 has a very obvious fade-out block in the second row. The red blocks in the quilt are like an afterthought. Perhaps four more blocks were necessary to make the quilt the desired size. You can see the stretching of the blues as far as they would go. Even a little black was added, but finally the quilter gave up and added the red. There wasn't quite enough, and this quiltmaker had to substitute.

When my mom first gave me this quilt, I fantasized how I would have taken the four odd red blocks and put one in each corner, or placed them in the safe and predictable center of the quilt. Fortunately, I wasn't able to do this. Living with the quilt has taught me that I always have to search for the red blocks, that is, I am forced to look at the quilt anew each time I open it for inspection. In the long run, all these peculiarities ultimately made the quilt more interesting.

There are numerous fade-out blocks in *Scrap Double T* on page 13. Block #6, Row #4 is uniformly lighter than the other blocks. Therefore, it also appears larger. Upon inspection of the quilt, it seems to be the quiltmaker's selection. Block #2, Row #6 is partially faded out, giving the viewer a different pattern to view. These differences appear to be caused by aging.

In Conclusion

So, there are specific things you can do to create a scrap quilt. My personal definition for a scrap quilt is:

1. It's made up of many different fabrics (no exact number).

2. The fabrics are used in a non-consistent way (all blocks don't match, but some cloning is allowable).

3. It must visually show from afar that different fabrics are used.

A house in San Francisco as viewed from across the street. It draws us toward it. Photo by Roberta Horton.

I haven't specifically discussed requirement #3, but it's really just a summary of what I've been saying. I was once led to a room in someone's home that featured many quilts being displayed. From the doorway where I stood, I couldn't identify the quilt above the mantle as being a scrap quilt. From my vantage, all the blocks looked identical. When I moved closer I noticed that a different brown fabric had been used to form each star. Unfortunately, all the fabrics were the same color of brown. The browns were exactly matched. This is a common tendency among quiltmakers, especially those that come from a clothing sewing background. Now, there are dark brown fabrics and light ones, bluer browns, and those that turn toward red. We tend to over-match when we should in reality be mis-matching.

What I'm really saying is that a good scrap quilt allows the viewer to see the differences: value, fabric pattern, color, and scale. A quilt should draw us toward it. As we get closer, we should be able to see additional things that weren't obvious from afar. There needs to be a reward for walking across the room to see the quilt at close range.

A closer inspection reveals a wonderful collection of teddy bears! Photo by Roberta Horton.

BUILDING A PIECED SCRAP QUILT

Sets

There are various configurations in which to assemble pieced blocks into a scrap quilt. Let's look at some blocks made during a Scrap Quilts workshop to illustrate the possibilities. After a fabric exchange, each participant ended up with four fabrics, not of their choosing. Three of the fabrics would be repeated elsewhere and one was unique to them. They were then required to make an Eight Pointed Star block using all four of their fabrics— a true scrap quilt!

Method I

The simplest configuration is to have all the blocks touch each other. Truth: scrap quilts tend to be busy because they often use many fabrics. The problem, then, is the multiplicity of visual stimuli which the maker needs to control. So, if the blocks are made from unrelated fabrics and randomly placed within the quilt, as in this example, they can fight for attention. The overall feeling is one of bedlam!

Method II

Strips of narrow sashing can be used to separate the pieced blocks into a grid. I have chosen a solid color because it would be more calming than a print. I have kept the blocks in the same order. Now, look at the blocks individually. You will notice that with this "breathing space" more blocks read as being acceptable. Having the blocks parallel to the outside edge of the quilt also exerts a calming effect.

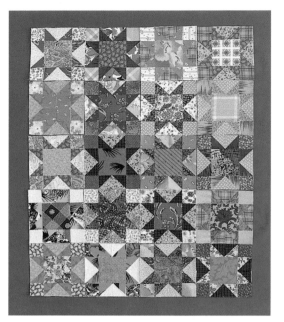

Method I. Blocks next to each other.

Method II. Blocks parallel to edge + sashing.

Method III

The blocks can be placed on point with sashing. Now the sashing presents strong diagonal lines. This set is busier than Method II for two reasons. Diagonal lines suggest movement, while parallel lines are static. Blocks on point also read busier and more mysterious because it's harder to see logically how they are constructed. To check this out, turn your head on the side and view the quilt. Immediately you should be able to understand how you would sew the blocks. Simple is calm, complicated reads as busy.

Methods IV and V

Plain blocks can be inserted between the pieced blocks. This option will give you twice as much quilt size for half as much work. The blank squares present a larger calm surface than the narrow strips of sashing, hence more dilution of activity. Having one color repeated across the surface of the quilt also calms it down. You'll notice that Method IV, with the blocks parallel to the edge of the quilt, is calmer than Method V, with the blocks on point. Remember the movement factor of diagonal lines.

Blocks made for any scrap quilt can be put through this auditioning process to determine the set. The answer to which arrangement is best won't always be the same. The determining factors are:

- the selected quilt block pattern
- the print or woven designs on the individual fabrics
- the number of different fabrics
- the number of different colors
- the scale of the print or woven designs on the fabric

Method III. Blocks on point + sashing.

Method IV. Blocks parallel to edge + plain alternate blocks.

You should have noticed that the quilt improved as either the sashing or plain blocks were added. You will find that Method V was the placement most commonly used by the makers of the antique quilts shown in this book.

I feel that Method I, where the blocks touch each other, is the approach that tests our creativity most. Using this method forces you to pay more attention to your individual fabrics.

Process for Methods I-V

1. Organize fabric into light, medium, and dark value piles. Ignore color. Check that there's a variety of fabric styles.

2. Select four lights, four mediums, and four darks. Don't pair up a particular light, medium, and dark in advance. Check for variety of color and fabric pattern in each value set. The natural tendency is to color coordinate. Don't do this, as it will result in a less interesting, more predictable quilt.

Method V. Blocks on point + plain alternate blocks.

Light, medium, and dark values.

Sets of mis-matched fabrics.

Sets of color-coordinated fabrics.

3. Cut the fabric shapes for four blocks and place them on the design wall. Rearrange within the four blocks until you're pleased with the relationship. Cut additional pieces if necessary.

Block #1	Block #2
Block #3	Block #4

Compose first four blocks.

4. Now add four more blocks to the composition. The fabric in each new block should be influenced by the already-composed blocks. Continue until the quilt is the desired size. The blocks aren't sewn until all of them have been composed.

Block #1	Block #2	Block #7
Block #3	Block #4	Block #8
Block #5	Block #6	

Compose four more blocks.

Let's look at an antique baby quilt containing only six blocks. Look at the first four blocks and how the fabrics relate to each other. Block #1, Row #1 and Block #2, Row #2 contain small brown prints which are fairly equal to each other. Block #2, Row #1 has a brown print which has a higher value contrast, making it appear stronger. Block #1, Row #2 has an eye-catching rust border stripe. It mis-matches and has the strongest print. When only the first four blocks are considered, this block is too different, too wild. It overwhelms the other three blocks. The blocks in the third row take care of the problem. Block #1, Row #3 contains a strong darker brown which stands up to the rust border stripe above it. They vie for attention. Block #2, Row #3 counter-balances the rust in color and gets the eye moving diagonally.

Method VI

Another choice for setting pieced units into a scrap quilt is to position them in rows. The antique *Strip Quilt* is composed with three different pieced units. These are then sewn into strips of matching units. This old scrap quilt is lovely in its simplicity. Notice how important the red and pink fabrics are. The units can also be separated by sashing. Examples are *Broken Dishes* page 59, *Passage From India* page 61, and *Chinese Coins* page 81.

Gem Block
27" x 41". Circa 1880-90. Collection of author. (Block pattern page 136)

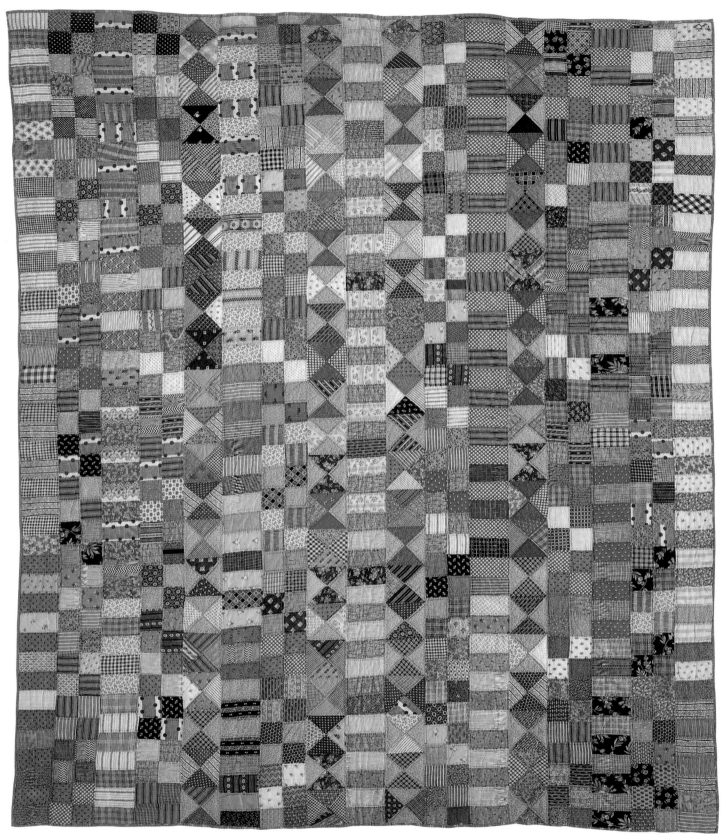

Strip Quilt
74" x 86". 1996. Circa 1890. Massachusetts. Collection of author.

Sixteen Patch Pinwheel
75" x 81". 1996. Mabry Benson, Kensington, California.

Method VII

A final choice would be to combine two blocks in a scrap quilt. Often a seemingly different pattern will emerge from the combination. *Sixteen Patch Pinwheel* on page 24 by Mabry Benson is a newly-made quilt inspired by an antique. Read across the top row to identify the two blocks. The old quilt proved too fragile for use and had to be retired. Mabry took the original 1890s quilt to a workshop taught by Barbara Brackman. She was delighted when Barbara pointed out that reproducing an old quilt was a legitimate way of preserving it.

Mabry went on a buying expedition to purchase the fabrics she thought she would need for her copy. She pinned together sets of fabrics that matched the original blocks. Later, she took the fabric sets (but not the original quilt) and her sewing machine along on a vacation. What you see is the result. The blocks were arranged according to whim. Mabry discovered that the feeling of diagonal lines could be exaggerated by alternating clockwise and counterclockwise pinwheels.

Placement of Unusual Fabrics

Let's scout out the places you can plug in unique fabrics in a scrap quilt. Keep in mind that interesting and/or large-scale fabrics don't necessarily cut up well into small pieces to be used within an individual pieced block. Their visual integrity is impaired if they are diced. Instead, save them for special handling.

Sashing

If a strong print is used for grid sashing (Methods II or III, pages 18-19), the perimeter background area of the pieced blocks must be calm. Or at least, most of them must be calm. Study *Square On A Square*. Some of the blocks feature strong stripes in the perimeter triangles. However, the majority are small prints and calm solids. The perimeter triangles are filled in with partial blocks. Note the change in pattern across the top of the quilt!

Quilts made in rows (Method VI, page 22) can also have a sashing inserted. *Passage From India* page 61 features a large-scale paisley wood block print for the sashing. The strips were cut so the patterns were lined up with each other for calmness. The triangle flying geese strips are composed of smaller-scale prints for the same reason.

Plain Alternate Blocks

When a bold or eye-catching fabric is used for the plain alternate blocks (Method IV or V, page 22), the pieced blocks must conversely be less interesting to view. Study *Shoo-fly* (page 27). Four printed border stripes and two large-scale fabrics have been used for the alternate blocks. Notice that the stripes are all on the same diagonal axis. Varying the grainline would create too much movement. Also note, however, that the matching fabrics are not cut identically throughout the quilt. Waste not, want not. This gives a more proper informal feeling to this scrap quilt.

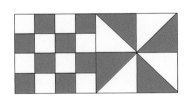

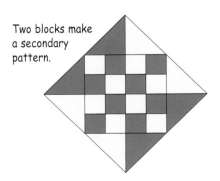

Two blocks make a secondary pattern.

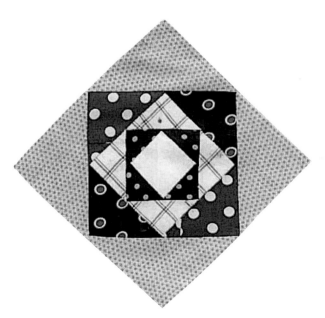

Detail of *Square On A Square*.

Square On A Square (top)
82" x 82". Circa 1880. Collection of author. (Block pattern page 136)

Shoo-fly (top)
70" x 70". Circa 1880. Collection of author. (Block pattern page 135)

Borders

Borders are a logical place to feature unusual fabrics. Remember that the busier the fabric, the calmer the interior of the quilt should be. Also keep in mind that since we're discussing scrap quilts, all four edges don't have to have the same fabric. They should probably be of similar value, though.

Backing

The backing of a quilt is another perfect place for unusual fabrics. Many antique quilts feature marvelous backing fabrics, although the maker may have just considered them out-of-fashion. For the timid at heart, it's an opportunity to showcase textiles you don't want to cut into smaller pieces. The backing is a great canvas for large-scale prints.

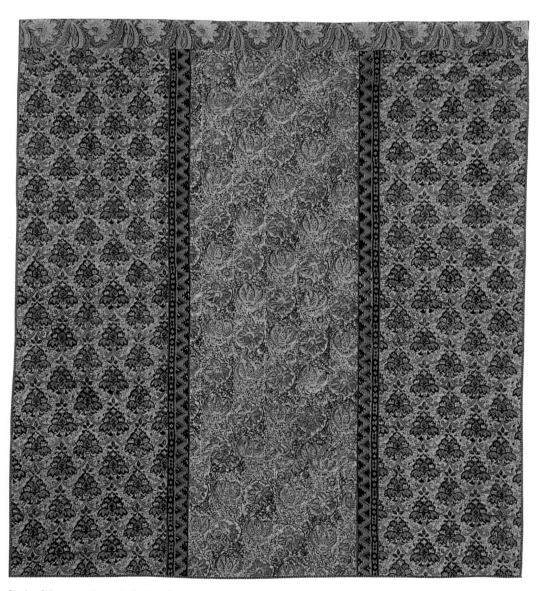

Back of *Passage From India*. For front view see page 61.

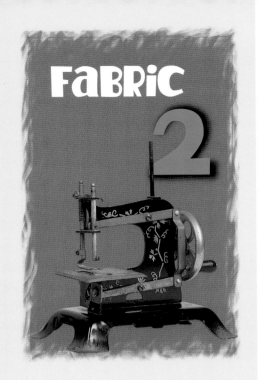

FABRIC

2

I just LOVE fabric! Being a quiltmaker gives me a legitimate reason to purchase fabric. The act of buying fabric at my local quilt store cheers me up if I'm depressed and fuels my creative juices if I am having a dry spell. I've been known to plan a trip to an exotic place around the need to track down fabric. It's all part of the game of building a fabric collection.

APPReciate YOUR FaBRic

One of my all-time favorite pieces of fabric is called *Les Travaux de la Manufacture* (The Activities of the Factory). This toile was designed by Jean-Baptiste Huet in 1783-84 and shows the process of printing fabric. It was commissioned by Christophe-Philippe Oberkampf, the owner of a textile printing factory in Juoy-en-Josas, France. Helen Grigg was fortunate to obtain a piece of this fabric, from which she made a whole cloth quilt, *Toile de Jouy*. The details from her quilt (page 30) show different aspects of the complex printing process. Helen added the printed explanations.

Toile de Jouy
50" x 63". 1990. Helen Grigg,
Lake Oswego, Oregon

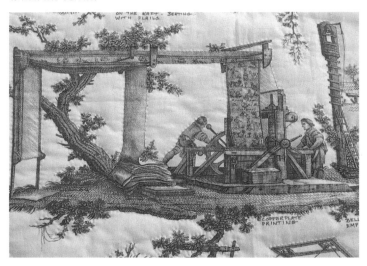

Block printing. First an outline block, followed by a block for each color within the outline.

Copper plate printing. Finer lines are possible in a single color print. (This fabric is an example.)

Most American quilters have had the experience of attending a "pot luck" dinner. Each invitee is to bring a food item that will be shared by the other attendees. Sometimes you're assigned a type of food, such as bread, salad, main course, or dessert. Other times, the hostess trusts to luck, and miraculously, the meal ends up being nutritionally balanced. Occasionally there are only desserts and everyone ends up with a sugar headache. Making a scrap quilt is based on the same idea. You want a balanced assortment of fabric choices for this smorgasbord of the quilt world.

Quilters tend to buy the same style of fabric over and over again. We all have preferences we favor and keep going back for more of that type. We ignore many fabrics because we don't understand their potential use, or flavor, in our quilts. Let's look objectively at some of the possibilities.

Fabric spread out in the meadow to dry and/or to whiten background.

The pencilers. Other colors are applied.

SMALL-SCALE PRINTS

Small-scale prints were the mainstay of antique quilts, although not the only choice, as some believe. You either love them (as many traditional-style quilters do) or are bored with them (as many contemporary-style quiltmakers are). What's important to understand is that they, like the other categories to follow, have their rightful place in scrap quilts. The premier quality of a small-scale print is that it's calming. Remember: Too many can be monotonous.

Florals

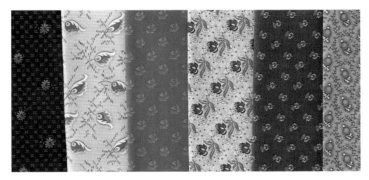

Floral: repeat

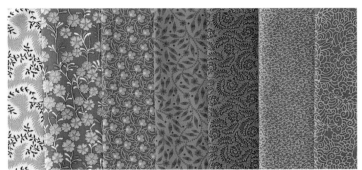

Floral: all-over

Puppy Dog Tails pattern by Judy Martin in her book *Judy Martin's Ultimate Book of Quilt Block Patterns* shows a combination of small-scale florals.

Northwind block also shows a combination of small-scale prints. (Block pattern page 135)

Geometrics

Geometrics is one of my all-time favorite categories.

Many quilters completely ignore it because the shapes are angular rather than sweet, like the florals. These tailored shapes fit easily in both traditional and contemporary quilts. They present a pleasing contrast to all other styles of fabric. (Also refer to Dots on page 42.)

Small-scale floral and geometric prints are available in a wide variety of patterns. Make sure to have some of each type for visual contrast.

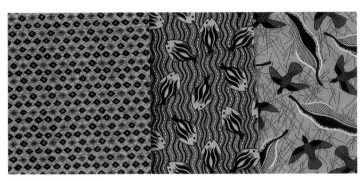

Geometric + busy African prints

Triangles, squares, and circles

Path Through the Woods block. Geometrics and stripes calm down large-scale, curved line designs.

Large-scale prints offer many choices of motifs.

Oregon Trail pattern by Judy Martin in her book *Judy Martin's Ultimate Book of Quilt Block Patterns.*

Large-scale Prints

Fabrics with large-scale designs are busy. Too many of them, too close together, give the viewer too much to see and are confusing. Large-scale motifs need to be paired with fabrics which are less important, such as small-scale prints or plaids and stripes. Solids and hand-dyes are also a way to dilute their busyness.

Study the Oregon Trail block. A large-scale Japanese figure is in the center square (its size determined the dimension of the 12" block). Notice how all the other fabrics are beautiful but less interesting. Two motifs are from the same fabric. Large-scale fabrics frequently have a change of subject matter within the design repeat which allows you to cut them up like Swiss cheese.

Large-scale prints demand that you select blocks which are big enough to showcase them properly. The King's Crown block has a multicolor, large, curving design in the center square. The orange batik dots mimic those in the central fabric; the corner batik repeats the leaf shapes. In both cases, the batik motifs are bigger than those found in the center fabric. However, they read as less busy because, more importantly, they have fewer colors.

Large-scale print + calming fabrics

King's Crown block (Block pattern page 136)

Large-scale, novelty print + calming patterns

Amish Star ➡ Quilter's Star (Block pattern page 137)

Let's look at a large-scale, multicolor novelty print. These are fun to buy but hard to cut up in a quilt and still keep the integrity of the design. It was necessary to cut the shapes individually, rather than randomly to eliminate confusion in the desired scenario. The snowflakes seem to be a diluting extension of the big print. A light blue stripe and a mottled green were the calming fabrics. I think this block needs to be re-christened. Quilter's Star seems a more appropriate name than Amish Star, since prints were used rather than the typical Amish solid-colored fabrics.

Large-scale prints are perfect for borders, backings, and sashings, because so much of the print will show in the large area. I recently purchased a large-scale, wood-block printed fabric and decided to use it for a glued mock-up I made to introduce some new plaids from my fabric line. I decided to create a Flying Geese set. I became so enamored with the mock-up that I was compelled to make the whole quilt (page 61). *Passage From India* differs from its inspiration because I didn't split the coloration of the two small triangles that frame the larger triangles in the flying geese strips. I needed the calmness of repetition because I was working with more fabrics.

Lastly, sometimes it's possible to visualize other shapes in large-scale prints. Study the gray tropical leaf fabric. Can you envision its use for cat fur?

Original glued mock-up

Detail of *Passage From India*.
For full quilt see page 61.

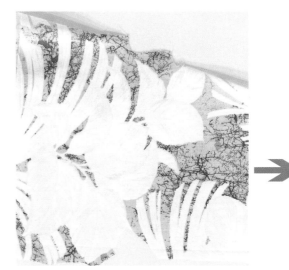

Large tropical print

Plaids and Stripes

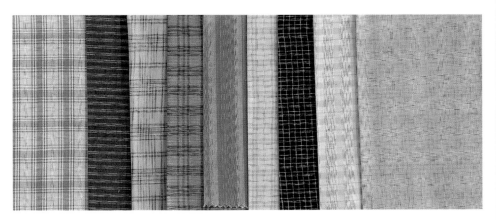

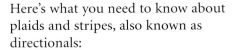

Ikats

A stripe positioned four ways.

Here's what you need to know about plaids and stripes, also known as directionals:

1. *Stripes* feature lines, or bars of color, going in only one direction. A stripe can be cut to be positioned four ways.

2. *Plaids* have lines going across, as well as up and down on the fabric. A plaid will read busier than a stripe because there's twice as much to see.

3. *Yarn dye* directionals have the pattern within the threads of the fabric itself, so it looks the same on both the right and wrong sides. It can be put on grain by pulling opposite ends to realign the threads or by washing (the fabric will relax in water and go back to its original woven shape).

4. *Printed* directionals will have brighter colors on the right side of the fabric. They have two grainlines. The visual grainline is the pattern you see. Unrelated to it is the physical grainline of the griege goods upon which the pattern is printed. When the two differ, go with the visual grainline. It's what others will see.

5. Plaids and stripes that run parallel to the edge of the quilt read as calm. Those at any other angle read as busy.

6. When an individual thread in the pattern contains two or more colors the resulting woven pattern is called an *ikat*. These patterns read as busier than if the individual threads are a single color. This is one of my favorite types of fabric, and I tend to use it a lot—a case of more to look at for your money.

Detail of *Pete's Place*. For full quilt see page 104.

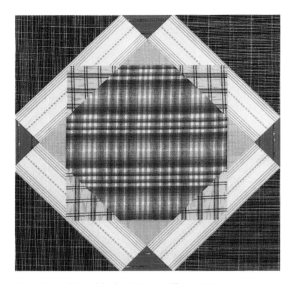

Union block. Interior illumination.

Hometown Hero block. Interior illumination.

7. Some plaids feature a special effect I have dubbed interior illumination. The medium and dark lines form a grid pattern which seems to float above the light background. This high value contrast gives a feeling of depth to this kind of plaid. They, therefore, are busier than other plaid designs. Flatter reading, less interesting fabrics should be used around interior illumination fabrics so they can show off properly.

8. When you are auditioning a plaid or stripe with a printed fabric, make sure to keep the directional pattern parallel to the edge of the table so it will be in its calm mode. This will allow you to see a better contrast between the two fabrics. In other words, don't fan out your fabrics when auditioning them.

Parallel = calm + busy

Diagonal = busy + busy

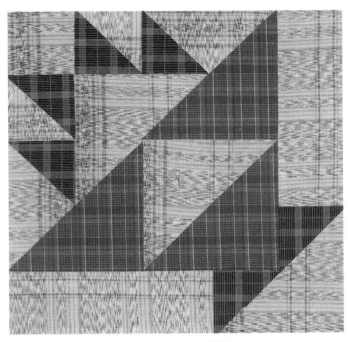

Flower Pot block #1 (Block pattern page 138)

9. Plaids and stripes will provide an excellent foil, or contrast, for any other printed fabric. Directionals allow you to see the other fabric better because the plaids and stripes read as calm. This is their job in antique quilts which are filled with plaids and stripes combined with other fabrics.

Let's look at four basket blocks which each contain some plaids and/or stripes. With the exception of the all-plaid Block #1, the baskets mix fabrics from various designers who work for different manufacturers. This guarantees an exciting mix of art styles and dye colors.

Block #1 is made solely of plaids. The complicated ikat light background gives a very antique feeling to the block. The pattern has awkward proportions which I enjoy.

Block #2 combines two traditional small prints with a plaid basket and a small light stripe for the background. Except for its red color, the fabrics in this block are the most calm.

Calm fabrics

Simple Flower Basket block #2 (Block pattern page 138)

Cake Stand block #3
(Block pattern page 138)

Block #3 combines a yellow-green plaid with a grey-green geometric. Notice that the green used for the leaves is different yet. This is a great example of color mis-matching rather than the dyed-to-match approach. An elegant marbleized yellow is used for the background, rather than the muslin that is typically used. All of these fabrics frame the sweet pansies—a most unusual combination of fabrics which I find very beautiful.

Block #4 features an unusual combination of fabrics. The large Japanese-feeling flower is made by Momen House. The purple leaf fabric is a Hoffman California Fabrics batik. The basket fabric is designed by Elly Sienkiewicz for her Baltimore Beauties™ Collection for P&B Textiles. The hand-woven, light ikat stripe is one of mine from the Clothworks Division of Fasco/Fabric Sales. Truly an eclectic collection of fabrics!

When I design a set of fabrics for a plaid collection, I purposely select patterns and colors that are different from each other. To my amazement, the unrelated collection can always be combined within a block. Because they don't go together, they can be used together.

Large-scale floral + dots + batik + ikat stripe

Fruit Basket block

Twelve fabrics

Twinkle Toes pattern by Judy Martin in her book *Patchworkbook*.

10. When you cut plaids and stripes, look at what you see:

a. There are lines on your fabric, lines on your ruler, and maybe, lines on your cutting mat. At least, turn your mat to the plain side.

b. When cutting individual shapes, use a template. If you cut using only your ruler as a guide, you will be looking at lines, through lines. A template allows you to place the ruler against the template, ignoring what you see through the ruler.

c. Layer four fabrics, then stack cut. You won't see the line patterns on three of the fabrics.

d. Scrap quilts are informal, so you don't have to be overly concerned with grainline. I favor "casually off grain" when working only with plaids. This means the results come out naturally, without you over-controlling the fabric. This is the look you will find in antique quilts. Remember, that's how you get energy into your quilt.

Look at some all-plaid and stripe quilts (pages 81, 82, 83, 85, 86, and 87) and see how it works.

Thirteen fabrics

Old Maid's Puzzle block (Block pattern page 138)

CHECKERBOARDS

Many companies have come out with checkerboard fabrics in recent years. I tend to buy as many different sizes, colors, and variations as I can. A checkerboard acts much like a plaid or stripe; that is, it provides a contrast to curved line designs. In some cases, large checkerboards give the appearance of having been pieced, particularly if you quilt on the lines.

Mabry Benson tried to find fabrics that duplicated those in a fabulous antique quilt top. Laying the top out, she tested candidates until she found ones that blended into the original. The fabrics aren't identical to the original, but they feel the same. The checkerboard Mabry used is to replace a large-scale, houndstooth plaid found in the original top. The result of her efforts is wonderful.

The checkerboard fabric, placed on point, is great in this quilt. It makes the quilt look even more complicated than it really is because each square looks like a miniature pieced block. Most quilters are awestruck when they see it. Mabry assures us, "The Lone Star was easy, though no one will believe me. They are all so convinced it is so hard that they don't even want to hear about it."

Detail of *Edy's Lone Star*

Edy's Lone Star
84" x 78". 1996. Mabry Benson, Kensington, California.

DOTS

Fairly early on in this current quilt revival, fabric manufacturers picked up on the fact that quilters represented a new market. They began to design textiles specifically for us. One of the first big hits were pin dots, which were a small polka dot printed in an even distribution. Once they proved popular, the pattern was issued in many colors. I remember seeing a quilt composed of only those pin dots. Even though many color versions were featured in the quilt, the size and spacing of the dots were identical. I diagnosed it as "pin dot over-kill." Color variation wasn't enough for visual interest.

The key to fabric usage is variation of pattern. If you limit yourself to a particular category, you must find variations within it. Study *Dots* by Nancy Freeman. Inspired by the name of a shop called Dots in Victoria, British Columbia, Canada, Nancy created this small appliqué composition. Almost all the fabrics feature dots of some kind, even six colors of the infamous pin dots that I previously mentioned. The trick is that Nancy had a nice dot collection.

Notice that Nancy used a few non-dot fabrics. They include a stripe, a plaid, and a checkerboard—all directional, linear patterns for a nice hard-edge contrast.

Nancy also used some of her dot fabrics in the quilt *Three Birds, Two Fish, And A Pot of Flowers* (page 109). Dots provide a wonderful contrast to other types of patterns. Small dots evenly distributed act as a calming geometric. Dots can convey a feeling of movement if they are large-scale, or if they are printed in an erratic fashion.

There are other unique shapes you can designate as a category in your fabric collection. Think of how many versions of stars, hearts, leaves, wood grains—even cats and dogs—you see in the marketplace.

Dots
18" x 14". 1997. Nancy Freeman, Benicia, California..

Stars arranged
from calm to busy

CHEATER CLOTH

Fabric printed to look like pieced patchwork patterns is called cheater cloth. A quilt made for the Centennial celebration of the United States used a cheater cloth as the backing. This is a perfect use for this type of fabric. Even earlier examples of cheater cloth fabric exist.

Two quilts in the Folk Art Quilts chapter have used cheater cloth. *Memories of Creeky Springs Ranch* (page 108) features it in the lower border. *Eklutna* (page 117) has a fake log cabin edging. Quilting in the printed seams will make it look more as though it was really sewn. Remember, keep your options open.

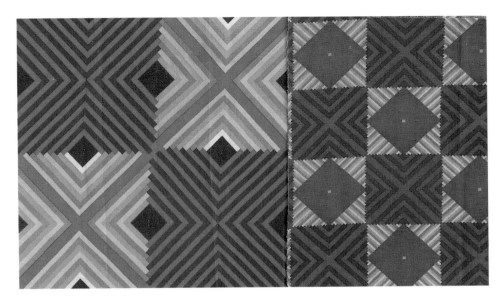

Cheater cloth

HAND-DYED FABRICS

Many textile dyers are making fabrics specifically with quilters in mind. Besides the mottled look, of which there are endless variations, there are also painted, marbleized, and air-brushed versions.

The use of hand-dyes in contemporary-style quilts is commonplace. Fewer people think of using them within a traditional-style quilt block.

Sometimes you can visualize shapes in the accidental patterns found in hand-dyes. I cut the bird directly out of a piece of marbleized fabric. The contour of the lines determined the shape.

Hand-dyed fabrics are often available at the merchant mall of quilt shows. Your local quilt store may also carry some, or refer to page 140 in the Buying Guide. Some commercial textile manufacturers are also producing fabrics with a hand-dyed look. Buy from numerous designers so you will have a wonderful collection of hand-dyes from which to select. Some enterprising quiltmakers are even choosing to create their own.

Detail of Pete's Place.
For full quilt see page 103.

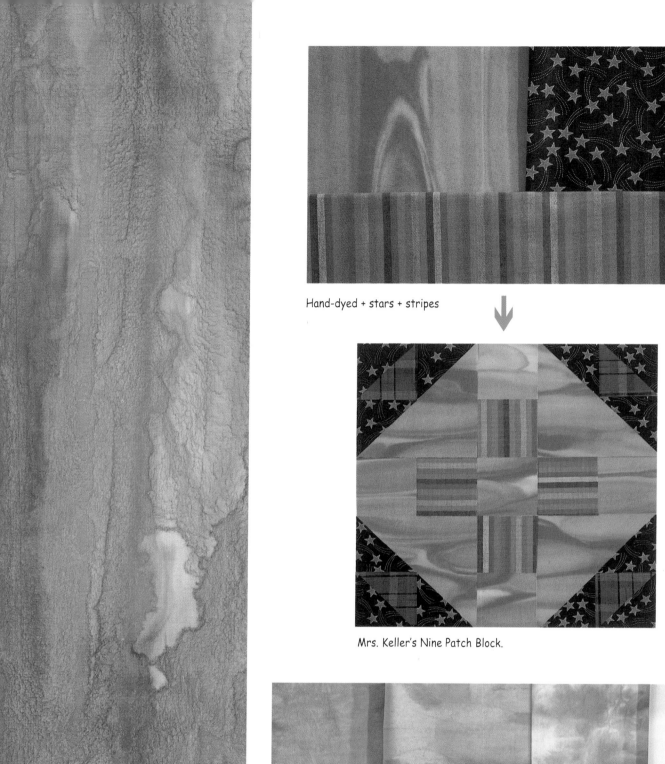

Hand-dyed + stars + stripes

Mrs. Keller's Nine Patch Block.

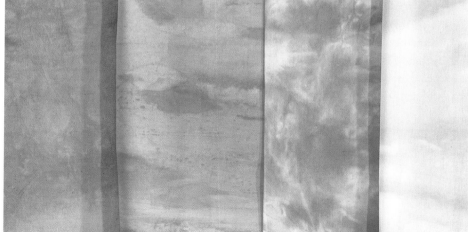

Mottled hand-dyes

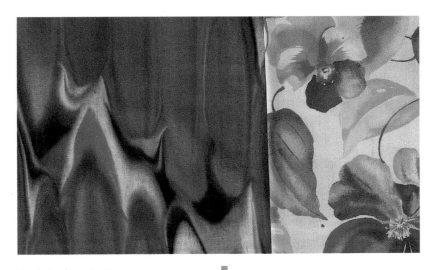

Hand-dyed + petunias

Fruit Basket block

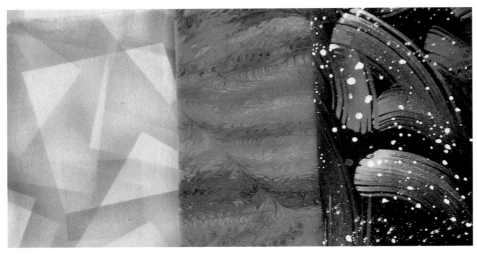

Airbrushed, marbleized, painted

Batiks

Batiks come in many styles, depending on the country of origin or the commercial company importing them. The design is created by placing a temporary wax on the fabric which will then resist the next dye bath. The results are more uneven, and alive, than if the fabric was merely printed. The irregularities give the fabric a hand-crafted look similar to wood-block printed fabrics.

Hoffman California Fabrics makes many colors and variations of a mottled batik that features designs which are created with a chop dipped in wax. The resulting fabric looks hand-dyed but will read as more busy because of the addition of motifs.

Study the first three selected fabrics above. The purple batik is intended to contrast with the larger, printed leaf fabric. The two fabrics differ in scale, value, and how the leaf motifs are drawn. The blue fabric was added to give a resting place for the eye.

The plaids were added because they are an unexpected choice to combine with the batik. Their straight lines allow you to better appreciate the curved lines of the leaf fabrics.

Batik + printed leaf + solid

Two plaids added

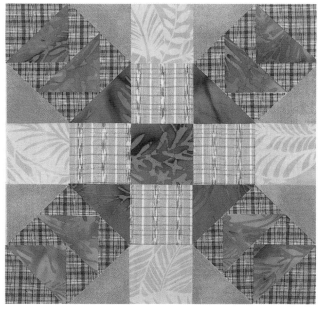

Wilderness Trail pattern by Judy Martin in her book *Scraps, Blocks & Quilts*.

Old copper batik chop

Sugar Bowl block

Union block (Block pattern page 137)

SKY

Many versions of sky fabrics are being printed. Each designer has a different way of saying the same thing. *Pete's Place* (page 103) and *Eklutna* (page 117) are landscapes, a logical use of such fabrics. Another advantage is that the fabric suggests the quilting pattern. Your quilting can follow the lines in the sky design. These fabrics can also be used in traditional blocks. An interesting feeling of depth or dimension is added by introducing a little sky fabric.

TEXTURE

Texture prints are easy to use. Their patterning is busier than a solid, but the shapes aren't identifiable, as a flower or a polka dot is. They have a more consistent surface patterning than a hand-dyed fabric. They offer a good contrast to the other categories already mentioned.

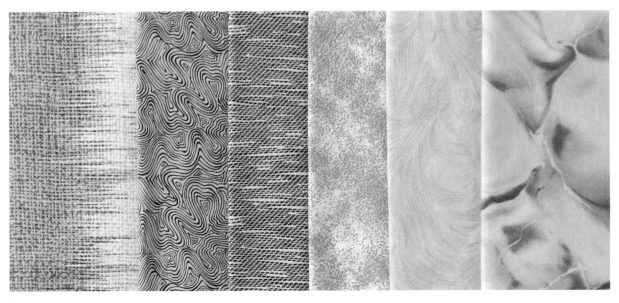

Texture prints

SUMMARY OF FABRIC CATEGORIES

In conclusion, learn to mix and match categories from a well-rounded fabric stash.

1. Pattern motifs need to contrast with each other in order to show off well in a quilt.

2. Not every fabric can be noteworthy—some only cover the batting. It all boils down to how calm or busy a fabric reads.

3. You want a good mix of flavors. Too many calms can prove boring, while too many choices from the busy side can be chaotic.

CALM	BUSY
SOLID	TEXTURE
SOLID	PRINTED MOTIF
TEXTURE	PRINTED MOTIF
SMALL-SCALE	LARGE-SCALE
GEOMETRIC	FLORAL
STRAIGHT LINES	CURVED LINES
DIRECTIONAL ON-GRAIN	PRINTED MOTIF
DIRECTIONAL ON-GRAIN	DIRECTIONAL OFF-GRAIN

COLOR

Fabric category is just one of the aspects to consider when you're selecting fabric for a quilt. Here are some other things to think about in your quest for making interesting blocks:

You may be comforted to know that you don't have to possess a vast knowledge of color and how it works to make a successful scrap quilt. Rep-etition of color seems to be more important than what colors, or color combination, you select.

For example, I frequently hear that yellow is a difficult color to use. I think instead we could just say that you see yellow when it's used in a quilt. It stands out, you look at it, so it's important to decide consciously where you're going to place it in the quilt. Study *Sunburst*. The yellow circles are used consistently for each block. Your eye sees the yellow and moves smoothly across the quilt. The eye-catching quality of yellow is negated because of repetition. If there was only one yellow center circle, then you would notice it!

Red is another color you notice in *Sunburst*. Red is used as the sashing. It's also used as an accent because it doesn't appear in every block. Red becomes the color that adds the spark to this quilt. You track it across the surface, but notice that this time your eye jumps rather than moves smoothly. Hence, red gives a touch of excitement. In this case, red is used as a conveyor to visually move you from one side of the quilt to the other.

Sunburst
82" x 88". 1870-80. Cordell, Oklahoma. Collection of author. Notice the half row.

If you ever have trouble with a color seemingly sticking out and being more noticeable than you want, try adding more of it. One spot of chartreuse (yellow-green) shows more than two or three. If the addition doesn't solve the problem, try removing it. If you're overcome with a sense of relief, it shouldn't be used in the quilt.

Another important color concept is that color needs to be mismatched. Look at the color wheel. You will see how one color bleeds, or moves, into the next one. In other words, there are versions of each color. For example, there's the pure version of red. There's also the red to which blue has been added that is called magenta, or red-violet. A red with added yellow becomes brick, or red-orange. There are hundreds of versions of red, and there may well be as many names, if we could just think of them. Have you read the names on lipstick tubes recently?

Quilters fall into the security of matching colors because they want their project to look good. A typical selection would be a light, medium, and dark value of one color. Instead, your goal should be to have many versions of a color which don't match each other. This will give an electricity to your blocks so each fabric can be seen and savored separately. Safe matching results in a homogenous blending that lacks vitality.

Birds in Flight is a brown quilt. Each block is composed of only three prints. The large triangle within each block is the same brown print throughout the whole quilt. As you inspect the smaller triangles, you will see many versions of brown. The browns reach over into rusty oranges. The coloration even branches out to include reds and yellows. Ofttimes there's an unexpected color in an old scrap quilt—a renegade. A renegade keeps the quilt from being too predictable. The renegade colors in this quilt are blue and green.

SUMMARY OF COLOR

In conclusion, remember these important things about color:

1. Repetition of color makes things go together.

2. Accent colors tell you where to look, move your eye across a quilt, and add excitement.

3. Colors need to be mismatched.

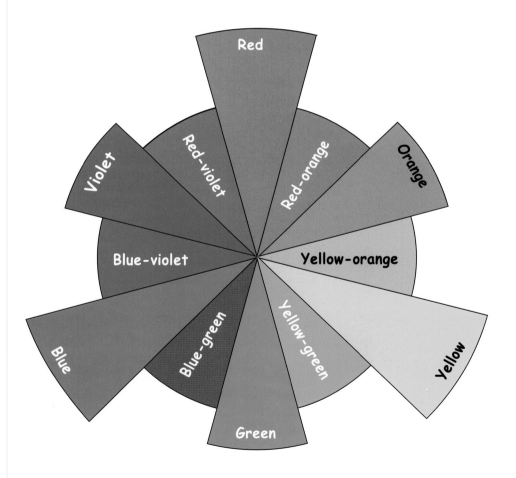

Color wheel

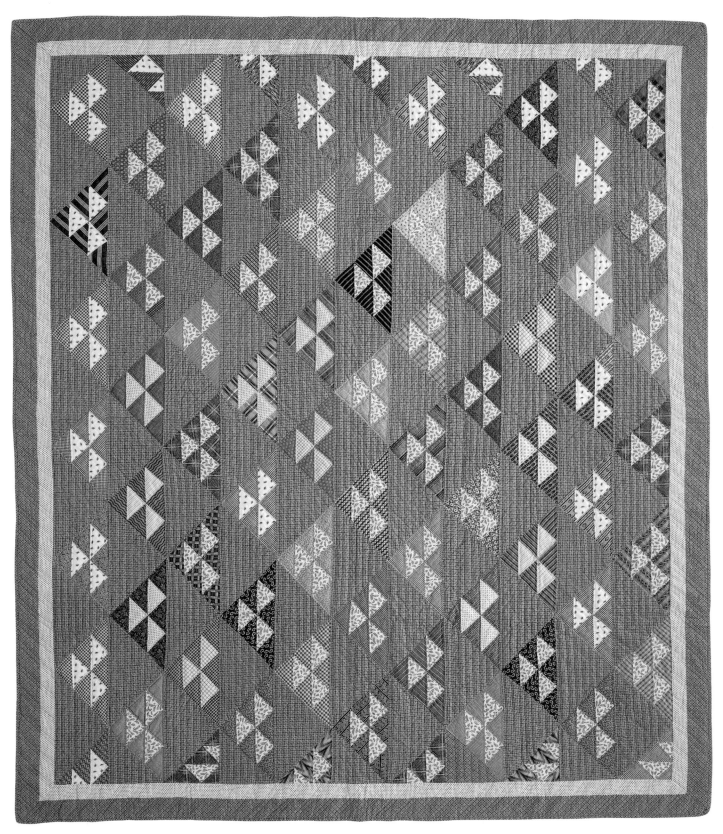

Birds in Flight
72" x 85". 1880. Elkhart County, Indiana. Collection of author. (Block pattern page 135)

value

Color is wonderful and fun to buy, but value is the true workhorse that gets the job done when you want to make a successful scrap quilt. Remember that value is how light or dark a fabric reads. Value contrast establishes the image you see. The difference in value pattern from block to block is what sets a scrap quilt apart from a repeated-fabric quilt. This is how you obtain the irregularities known as variations. The differences from block to block are the signals that tell you that you're looking at a scrap quilt.

Savor the wonderful use of value shading in *Sunburst* on page 49. Block #2, Row #4 comes closest to being a two-value block of light and dark even though more than two fabrics are used within the unit. Block #3, Row #2 and Block #2, Row #3 nearly duplicate this value

pattern. All the rest of the blocks feature a more random placement of value. Once again, every single block must be inspected. Notice that the light triangular wedges help to move your eye through the quilt. This is good to know for those quiltmakers who are afraid of white. Your eye sees it and therefore will look for more of it.

Those blocks with the most value contrast appear to be the busiest. Block #1, Row #2 has a high degree of activity. Compare this level of activity with Block #3, Row #3. This block almost fades out because of the low value contrasts. It's the quiet, restful spot. Notice how this block also appears smaller than Block #3, Row #2 directly above it. Remember that light reads larger.

Let's look at two blocks from *Edy's Lone Star* page 41 by Mabry Benson. Compare Block #3, Row #1 with Block #1, Row #4 in the detail photos here. If you squint and look at the two blocks, you'll notice that the center star areas read very differently

from each other. In one block you can see the pink triangular spikes; in the other star, the spikes fade into the background. Also look at the diamonds that form the outer circle within the star. One block uses one matching fabric for all these diamonds while the other uses two fabrics that read as one.

SUMMARY OF VALUE

In conclusion, value performs three important jobs in a scrap quilt:

1. Value contrast defines the shapes or images you see.

2. Value helps to determine the level of activity within a block or within a zone of the quilt.

3. Value can change the perceived size of a unit.

Details of Edy's Lone Star. For full quilt see page 41.

PROPORTION

Many quiltmakers are only concerned about the finished size of a pieced block. Perhaps the size is convenient to making the finished quilt the desired size. Or, maybe they have a set of commercial templates that will produce a particular size block. When your goal is to make your fabric show well within a quilt, the size of the individual geometric shapes within a pieced block is even more important than the finished size of a block. A geometric shape must be large enough to show the fabric motif or design well. Too large a shape can overwhelm the fabric. Sometimes it may be necessary to choose a different block with larger or smaller pieces to accomodate the fabric.

I suggest that you draft out the selected block in several sizes. This will let you see realistically how big the individual shapes are. If need be, make a white paper window template for the various geometric shapes (don't include seam allowance). This can then be placed on the fabrics you're auditioning. Check to see if enough of the fabric pattern will show. You will discover that this is more important for the larger-scale prints. Smaller-scale fabrics seem to look alike, no matter what the template size is.

The Album pattern below was done as a 12" block using three fabrics. The purple plaid appears too over-

Window templates used to determine correct size shape for fabric.

bearing when you see 4" squares of it. One option would be to make a smaller version of the block.

Another option was to select another 12" block that contained smaller geometric shapes which reduced the purple plaid to a 3" square. The Square Surrounded block can be done as a two fabric block using only a dark and a light fabric, but I decided to be more adventuresome. The original yellow plaid combined with the purple fern fabric was restricted to the flying geese cross bar. This gave a focus. I also decided to add other versions of yellow in the corner sections. Since yellow is so visible, the trick is to add different versions of a troublesome color. I find the finished block much more complex and exciting than the original attempt.

Album block (Block pattern page 137)

Square Surrounded block

MOOD

A particular combination of fabrics can convey the feeling or mood of a quilt. In other words, you can select a personality for your quilt as part of your initial recipe. Let's look at one fabric used in two different blocks. Notice the mood change between the blocks.

The House block is done all in plaids. It has a warm, folksy feeling, like an old log cabin. The red and green stripe feels informal.

The Path Through the Woods block feels much more elegant. I first contrasted two small-scale geometric fabrics with a larger-scale leafy floral. These Liberty™ fabrics were then combined with three plaids/stripes. See how different the red and green stripe feels in this block. Now it has the appearance of taffeta, and reminds me of an English country manor house. I can almost hear the crunch of gravel as a car or horse-drawn carriage moves along the driveway!

Log cabin in Canada. Photo by Roberta Horton.

House block

Path Through the Woods block

Country manor house in England. Photo by Roberta Horton.

TEMPERATURE

The overall feeling of temperature can most easily be controlled through the use of your white fabrics. Pure white fabrics read as cold, and off-whites read as warm. I enjoy mixing my white fabrics in the light area of a pieced block. Study the Gentleman's Fancy block. The light stripe is a warm off-white, but purposely isn't a perfect match for the still warmer light beige found in the large leaf. I then selected a colder white uneven checkerboard print to act as a foil in both temperature and pattern for the other fabrics. Three of the fabrics in the block feel warm while one is cold. This gives more visual interest to what is basically a two-color block.

Our Village Green block uses two lights. One is darker and warmer than the other. The lighter, cooler triangles come toward you in this block, adding a feeling of dimension. Your eye will go to the lightest fabric first. Here I used the whitest lights as stepping stones to move you around within the all-plaid block.

CONCLUSION

A quiltmaker has many things to think about when composing a scrap quilt. First she must select the categories of fabrics to be combined as well as the color range and desired mood. When a block has been selected, the correct proportions must be determined. Value placement within individual blocks will reveal the pattern and variations. Even more important is the value arrangement throughout the quilt. Scrap quilts require a lot of thinking because there are so many choices to be made. But then, that's why they are so much fun to live with when they're finished. Revel in your options!

Our Village Green block

Three warm + one cool fabric

Gentleman's Fancy block (Block pattern page 137)

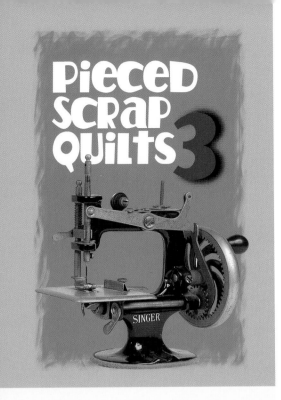

PIECED SCRAP QUILTS 3

It takes more time to design a scrap quilt than a repeat fabric quilt because there are many more choices to be made. Of course, I think making the decisions is the fun part! I love discovering that one combination works better than another, or, that I have the power to enliven or dull down an area. For me the reward of having a wonderful and interesting quilt outweighs the extra time it took to make it.

BLOCK POSSIBILITIES

Sometimes scrap quilts take more time to sew because you won't always be able to use a speed technique—what has come to be known as power sewing. With thought, sometimes a speed technique can be adapted to make allowances for your fabric variations.

In most cases, you can at least cut more than one shape at a time by employing stack cutting. Stack either four layers of the same fabric or four layers of four different fabrics. Iron to temporarily glue them together; then cut. Sometimes shapes can be cut first as a strip, and then, using special rulers, cut into separate template shapes.

Any pieced block can probably be used for a scrap quilt. Select one that will allow you to play some games. Can the block be done as both a two-value and a three-value block? Is it possible to create variations of the pattern by changing the value placement within the block? Even if all the blocks are built the same way, the fabric changes from block to block will turn it into a scrap quilt.

So, let's look at some quilt patterns which have been made into scrap quilts and explore the possibilities.

BROKEN DISHES

There are various ways to set a quilt. Let's compare one pattern used two different ways. *Roberta's Broken Dishes* (page 58) by Marie-Christine Flocard uses the simple pieced pattern block set parallel to the edge of the quilt. Plain alternate blocks are added. However, her quilt doesn't have the usual checkerboard format because identical fabrics are positioned diagonally in the alternate plain blocks. Notice how the large-scale stripes are positioned to emphasize the diagonal feeling.

Now compare the busyness in the areas where the larger-scale plaid is used in the alternate blocks with the quietness of the areas where small-scale, low-value contrast fabrics are used. The activity level doesn't have to be uniform throughout a scrap quilt. Did you also notice that there are some fade-out Broken Dishes? This quilt is made entirely of plaids and stripes.

Detail of *Roberta's Broken Dishes*

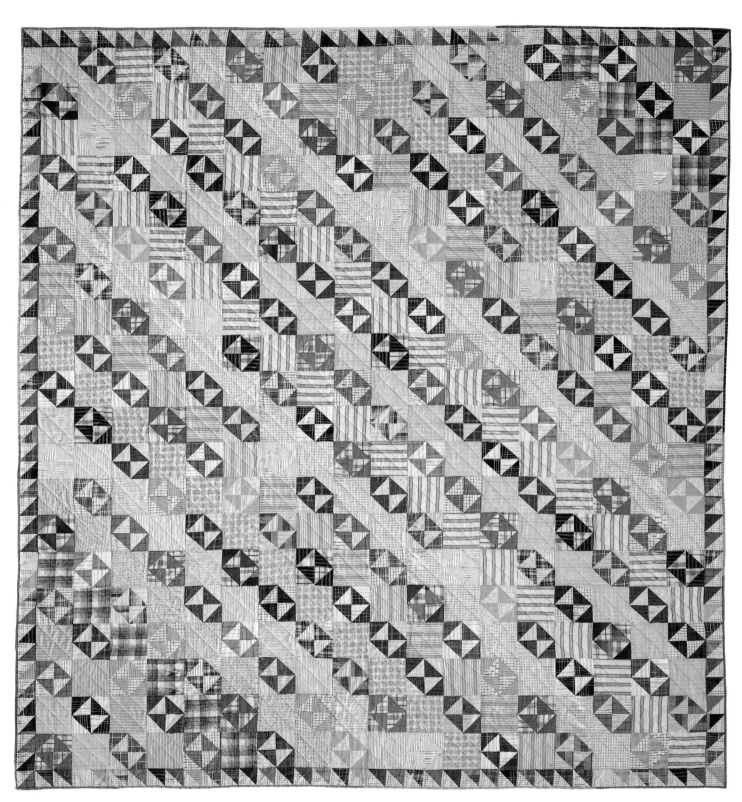

Roberta's Broken Dishes
76" x 86". 1996. Marie-Christine Flocard, les Loges en Josas, France. (Block pattern page 135)

Nadi Lane set her Broken Dishes blocks on point in rows that are at a 45-degree angle to the edge of the quilt. When the individual blocks were finished, they felt too dark and busy. Nadi's solution was to add lights and mediums for the setting triangles. Remember, these plaid and stripe triangles will be viewed as less interesting visually than the prints used within the blocks themselves. This, in turn, emphasizes their secondary role in the quilt.

A dark printed floral stripe is used for the sashing. Note that Nadi didn't cut all the strips identically. Once again, this tends to emphasize the scrap feeling of the quilt.

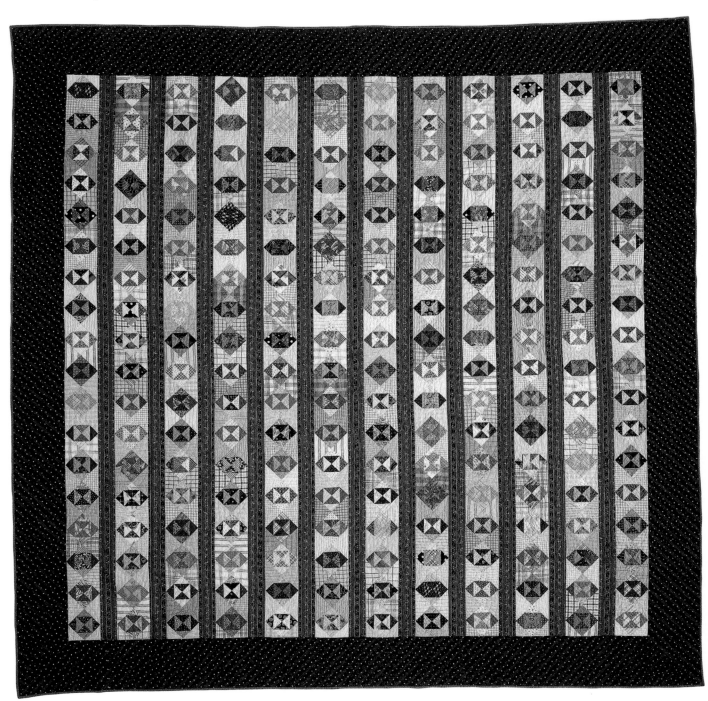

Broken Dishes
104" x 104". 1994. Nadi Lane, Agoura, California. (Block pattern page 135)

FLYING GEESE OR WILD GOOSE CHASE

My *Passage From India* uses Flying Geese set into rows. The important fabrics are hand-block printed in India. Plaids and stripes are added as a foil. A large-scale floral/paisley with a linear feeling was selected for the four central sashes, while a smaller-scale vine resides on the two outside sashes. Two different large-scale prints featuring flowers form the borders. I was aiming for this quilt to feel antique, perhaps from the 1840 era.

Notice the variation in value of the larger light triangles in the Flying Geese strips. This value change should help you to see that I elected to work in clusters of cloned blocks. Much of my fabric in the quilt was large scale with curving lines which gave a feeling of movement. This repetition of units was to add calmness.

The red triangles are the accents. Their spacing became the most important issue in composing the quilt. Originally the quilt was one row narrower and four units shorter. After agonizing for several days, I finally made it larger than my original plan. I just wanted, and needed, to see more of it.

Wood blocks (numbers denote pattern) and fabric printed from wood blocks.

Note: A wood block erroneously placed upside down.

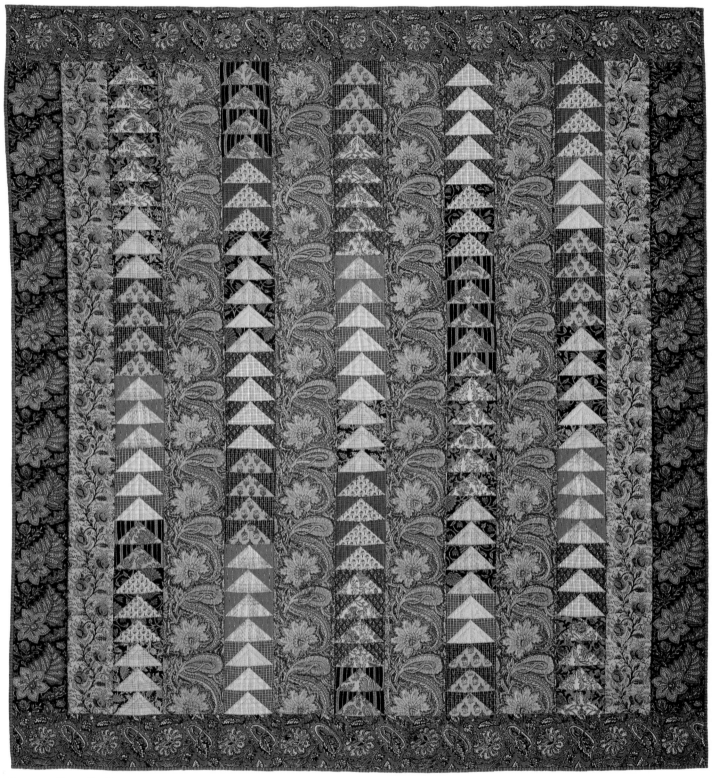

Passage From India
68" x 77". 1996. Roberta Horton, Berkeley, California. Quilted by Janet Dollard.

Which Way South?
65" x 68". 1996. Gwyneth McMillan, Albany, California. Collection of Lea Lopez, Tarzana, California.

Which Way South? by Gwen McMillan showcases a contemporary arrangement for Flying Geese. Gwen set out to create a sunrise or a sunset. On her design wall she arranged straight strips of the appropriate colors—and was displeased with the result. At some point Gwen realized that she could change the angles of her strips, and *voilá*, the quilt was born. Notice that Gwen has zones of color, with the yellows being mainly concentrated at the top of the quilt. Several of the strips have a fade-out quality.

Wild Goose Chase
71" x 83". Circa 1880. Collection of author.

Flying Geese can also be set to form a diagonal grid. The pattern is then sometimes called Odd Fellows or Wild Goose Chase. The first example isn't made from scraps. It's graphic and very straightforward. All the fabrics are prints, but age has reduced some, particularly the green within the quilt, to almost a solid, at most a tone-on-tone. Two different small-scale, light prints are used for the small triangles of the geese strips. This situation would keep some quiltmakers of today up all night fretting that they ran out of fabric. The fabric substitution isn't enough to move this quilt into the scrap category because visually, from afar, the two fabrics still read as if they are identical.

Wild Goose Chase
67" x 79". Circa 1890. Collection of author.

For contrast, the second *Wild Goose Chase* is a scrap quilt. It truly does take longer to read this pastel quilt. The totally random arrangement of the many fabrics works well with the white blocks. Some of the tiny fragments have lost their original color, so some wonderful interruptions in pattern exist. Note this particularly in the borders, where the geese seemingly hop and skip along.

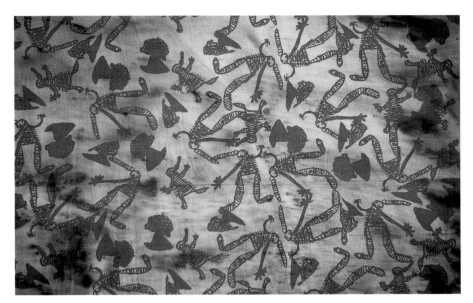

Important fabric

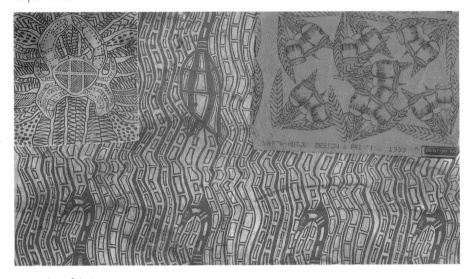

Secondary fabrics

Extender fabrics

An antique New Jersey quilt similar to the two previous quilts inspired me to create *Corroboree* (page 67). That is, the set formation made me realize that the geese strips could be used as a sashing to surround some interesting fabric, rather than the white used in the previous two quilts.

Here was my problem: I had collected some silkscreened Aboriginal-designed fabric from the Warta-Kutju Project in Kalgoorlie, Western Australia. I wanted to keep one larger piece of fabric that depicted little girls intact, or at least in big chunks. The elderly designer told me that this was her memory of attending a *corroboree*, or gathering, as a child. Food was eaten, tales were told, and songs and dancing filled the night. This fabric could be used for the large squares. I had to experiment to determine the appropriate size so enough subject matter showed and the measurement would work out okay for the drafting of the geese blocks.

I didn't mind cutting up some of the Aboriginal fabrics into small triangles because I didn't like certain of the designs in their entirety. I also had only small quantities of some of these fabrics. These fabrics could be used in the geese strips.

Naturally, I ran out of Australian fabric when I made the quilt, so I had to add some inconsequential fabrics to fill in the holes in the geese strips. Basically they are hand-dyes, textures, and circles (a motif seen in a lot of Australian Aboriginal art).

Audition arrangement of geese

Pivotal fabric added

The quilt was composed in separate stages:

1. Geese units for the entire quilt were composed on my design wall according to color and fabric choice. Each strip of four units of geese repeats the fabric.

2. The geese units were sewn and joined into an easily moved strip.

3. I experimented with the direction of the geese strips, trying random, consistent, and up and down arrangements. I selected the calmest version.

4. Squares and perimeter triangles were positioned.

5. Posts were added.

The finished size of the quilt was determined by the amount of fabric I had, the fabric with little girls on it being the main limiting factor. This quilt is finished off with a green stripe binding. It seemed to seal the composition nicely. I also auditioned red, but it called too much attention to itself. The overall challenge for me in this quilt was to use a traditional format with the unusual fabric and still keep the spontaneity and exuberance of the Aboriginal textiles.

Corroboree
50" x 50". 1995. Roberta Horton, Berkeley, California. Machine quilted by George Taylor, hand quilted by Roberta Horton.

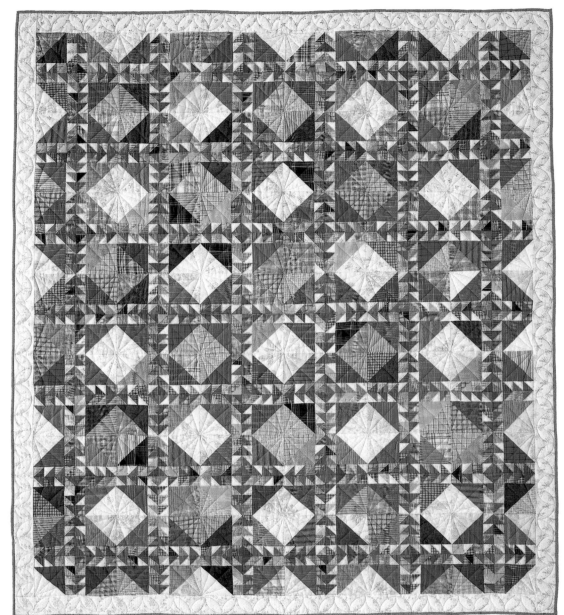

Morning Mist
65" x 75". 1996. Willemke Vidinic, Paris, France.

Lend and Borrow block

Morning Mist by Willemke Vidinic is a Lend and Borrow, or a variation of Lady of the Lakes. Four blocks form a cross. The resulting Flying Geese sash is parallel to the edge. In contrast to the other quilts shown in this section, the Flying Geese are formed from half-of-a-square triangles that come together when two blocks abut. Visually you see the sashes surrounding Diamond in a Square.

Willemke used traditional-feeling plaids and prints for this beautiful antique-feeling quilt. Pink is the renegade color. Notice that there is an alternate lighter/darker checkerboard rhythm. Large triangles of prints are in the light areas and large triangles of plaids are in the darker areas. Look for the exceptions.

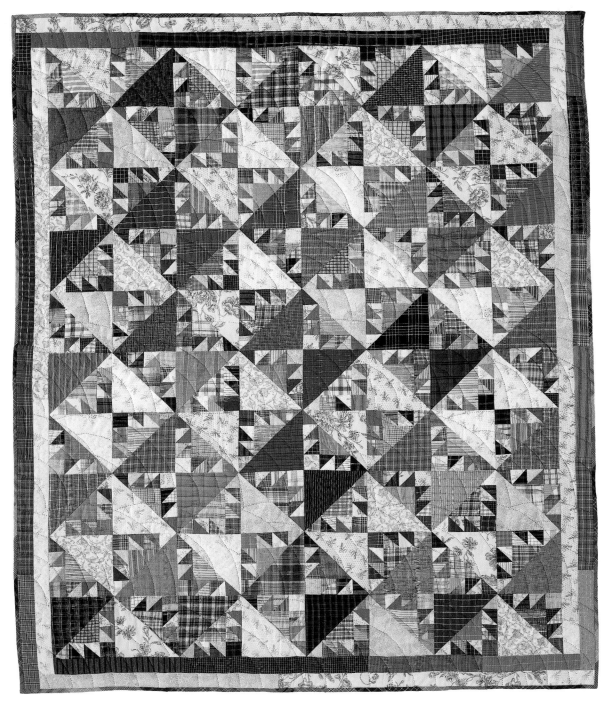

Delectable Mountains
54" x 66". 1996. Anne Walker, Epson, Surrey, United Kingdom. (Block pattern page 136)

DELECTABLE MOUNTAINS

Delectable Mountains by Ann Walker elegantly combines plaids with prints. Four blocks join to form a pinwheel, with two opposite large triangles being light and two being medium/dark. The large lights are all prints in a variety of tones and designs. The plaids really allow these prints to show well. The quilt is bordered in a very unique way. Large overlapping quilted fans skim over the surface of the quilt.

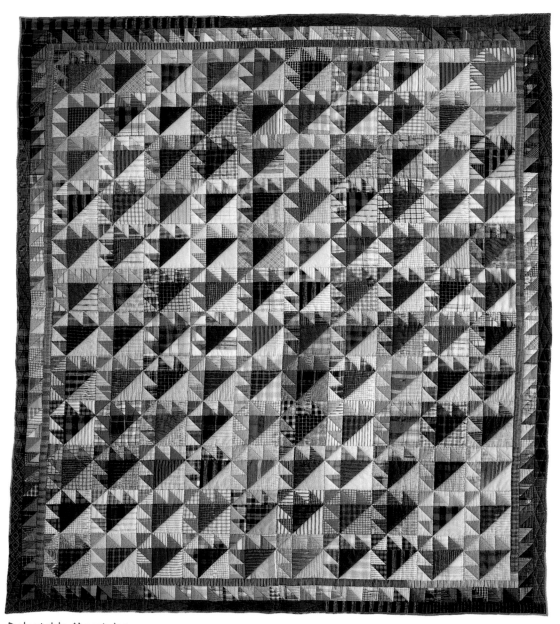

Delectable Mountains
87" x 102". 1995. Carroll Griffiths, Modesto, California. (Block pattern page 136)

Delectable Mountains by Carroll Griffiths is made totally from plaids and stripes, which gives the pattern a very different look. Carroll selected this block because she particularly liked the positive and negative space pattern that emerges. Wanting to keep the look clean and tailored, Carroll elected to orient her blocks in the simplest way.

Carroll wanted to use as wide a variety of plaids and stripes as possible for her scrap quilt. She particularly looked for bright versions. A kind friend gave Carroll some plaids from the 1970s. Carroll says, "I caught myself really eying people's plaid clothing in public places, wondering if they would miss a hunk cut out! I managed to control myself."

The center composition was first framed in a random striped inner border; then triangles were added. Carroll placed the darkest triangle combinations at the corners and gradually lightened them toward the center of each side. A wider, random-pieced strip surrounds the triangles. Finally, a random-cut bias binding was added. The quilt was hand quilted during a Mennonite quilting bee, using a thick batting, for a nice puffy feeling.

Turning a New Leaf
50" x 36". 1997. Deborah Altfeld, Atwater, California.

Debby Altfeld has christened her quilt *Turning a New Leaf* because she feels that she learned to see and appreciate her fabrics with new eyes as the result of a 5-day workshop retreat I taught. Her block is really like the previous two quilts, except that Debby has added an appliquéd stem to transform the pattern into a leaf shape. Three of the shapes are turned in the opposite direction, which adds an element of surprise for the astute viewer.

Three to four fabrics were used per block. Block #7, Row #3 has triangles that almost fade into the background. Look how the yellows and oranges have been sprinkled through the quilt. Debby has used a full range of fabric motifs. Some selections are repeated, the second time with another set of partners. Most of the fabric pairings within a block aren't obvious choices. Amazingly, they all go together!

No formal border was used. Three fabrics have been used in the binding. As Debby ran out of one, she switched to the next one. The quilt was machine stitched in the ditch along the joining seams of the blocks. The interior of the blocks, where the work shows, was hand quilted 1/4" from the seams. A special motif was placed in the large triangle part of the leaves.

Debby says, "With this quilt I learned to stretch my boundaries and try things I hadn't done before. As the quilt developed, I got a sense of what I wanted to do next. I was also challenged by a fellow classmate to include fabrics I considered 'dog' pieces. They actually ended up in the quilt, and I'm pleased with their effect."

Dolly's Quilt
20" x 26". 1925. Collection of Nancyann Twelker, Shoreline, Washington.
(Block pattern page 138)

Baskets

There are many basket quilt blocks. Let me start with the delightful *Dolly's Quilt* owned by Nancyann Twelker. What is so appealing to me is the fact that I've never seen this variation before. I love the awkward proportions of this five-patch. Due to the fade-out factor, the interior chips are read numerous ways. For example, compare Block #2, Row #1 with Block #1, Row #2. There are, in fact, four ways to read the six blocks value-wise. Viewed from afar, the quilt seems to contain about seven different fabrics, although twenty-one have actually been used. This turn-of-the-century quilt includes a double pink in the plain alternate blocks, cadet blue, and even a black mourning print (Block #3, Row #4).

Mennonite Baskets
38" x 46". 1880. Collection of author.

Mennonite Baskets is another five-patch block. This baby quilt is rendered in a typical Pennsylvania coloration. The quilt joyfully embraces all the variations inherent in the pattern—no two blocks read alike. Compare Block #1, Row #1 with Block #3, Row #1. Block #2, Row #4 is my personal favorite because it showcases both of the previous variations. This quilt has a fair share of "dog" blocks! It spoke to me from a gallery wall and made me buy it. I find it totally charming.

Some fabrics are repeated, partnered the next time in a new combination. Other fabrics make a solo appearance. For example, two distinctly different yellows are in Block #2, Row #3. This quiltmaker definitely didn't make pretty, well-defined blocks. How then does the quilt work? Why do all these blocks seem to fit into a quilt successfully? The answer is repetition. The same strong, small-scale red print is used for the plain alternate blocks, perimeter triangles and outer border. The same green appears in the inner border, corner blocks, and binding. This adds stability to the chaos of the blocks, tieing them together into a pleasing whole.

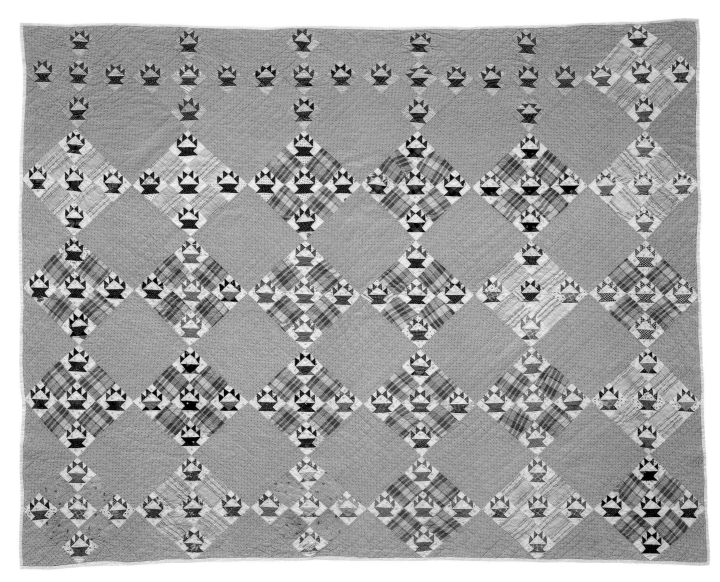

Mini Cake Stand in a Nine-Patch
1910. 79" x 66" Collection of author. (Block pattern page 138)

Mini Cake Stand in a Nine-Patch is a full-size quilt, but the individual four-patch basket blocks are only 3". Four different fabrics are used for the unpieced squares in the nine-patch units. Notice the random and unpredictable way the block units are laid out in the quilt. The blue baskets in the first row are paired with the same pink fabric that is used for the plain alternate blocks. All you see in these units, then, are the baskets themselves. They appear to float across the top of the quilt.

The most important fabric visually in this quilt is the maroon plaid joining fabric. It surely is the most eye-catching! Note that several of these plaid squares are patched. The patching shows because the plaid pattern is off-set at the joining seam. Not all of the plaid is cut on-grain. The total quilt doesn't appear too busy, however, because half of the quilt is the small-scale pink fabric, which reads as a solid. Remember, solids are calming. Notice that this antique quilt from Tennessee has no borders. Nor does it need them.

Close inspection of *Mini Cake Stand* reveals that many fabrics were used to compose the baskets themselves. Block #1, Row #1 is the most predictable in fabric usage. I would guess it was the first unit constructed and the quilter loosened up as she went along. Because individual fabric pieces are so small many liberties could be taken with grainline, etc., and the blocks wouldn't become too busy. The quilt is a real treat to read.

Cake Crumbs
63" x 78". 1997. George Taylor, Anchorage, Alaska. (Block pattern page 138)

Cake Crumbs by George Taylor is a contemporary version of Cake Stand. As the name might imply, the blocks are rejects from another larger quilt. George's goal was to see if he could indeed combine these seemingly unrelated baskets.

The total range of fabrics span the spectrum of all the types available to a present-day quilter: geometrics, polka dots, plaids, reproduction, marbleized, florals, and textures. The most difficult to sneak in are the currently popular large-scale, high value contrast, multicolor prints. The basket fabric, in most cases, was then combined with a fairly quiet background. Sometimes a third fabric was added in the large background triangle. No substitutions were employed within the blocks themselves, contrary to what was done in *Mini Cake Stand* on page 74. Even with this calming repetition, there is a high percentage of "dog blocks."

George elected to set the blocks next to each other on point. No plain alternate blocks are used to dissipate the energy of the fabrics. What makes the quilt work are the variations in how the blocks are interpreted. George's formula included:

1. blocks with a strong value contrast (boring but they anchor the more flimsy baskets)

2. fade-out blocks

3. blocks in which part of the basket seems to disappear

4. reversal to darker background, lighter basket in some places

5. use of yellow as a renegade in this mostly pink and green quilt

The composition is then framed by a sawtooth border which pulls everything together. Look for the reversals in direction of the triangles. Initially all the changes were positioned at the predictable mid-point on each side. George was urged to get off of "autopilot" because this is, indeed, an informal scrap quilt. The triangles contain fabrics from both basket quilts George has made. A simple grid is machine quilted over the surface of the quilt. The effect is reminiscent of the machine grids placed on some utility quilts. A friend refers to this as "Treadle Quilting."

Detail of *Cake Crumbs*

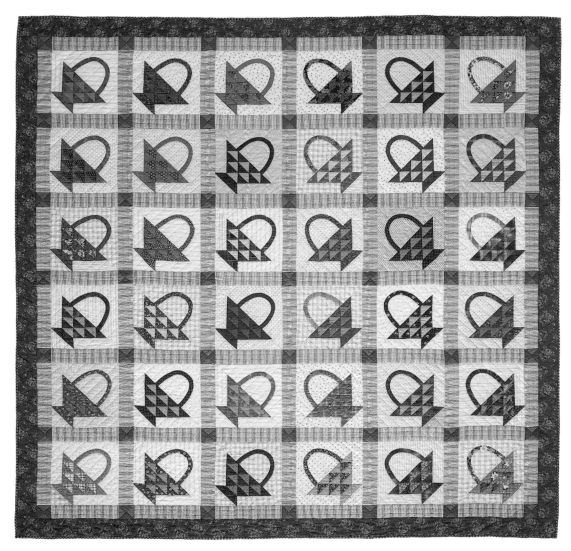

Nancy's Berry Baskets
81" x 82". 1995. Barbara Dallas, Portland, Oregon. Collection of Nancy Robb, Oakland, California.

Nancy's Berry Baskets by Barbara Dallas uses a basket drawn in a six-patch, more commonly called a nine-patch grid. The handles were hand appliquéd, using a freezer paper technique, to ensure their accuracy. The basket blocks are set parallel to the edge and are divided with a medium-value stripe sashing, which also rims the quilt in an inner border fashion. A stabilizing pieced dark cornerstone appears at the intersections. The framing is completed by a dark outer border.

Each basket is constructed from two fabrics. No two blocks pair the same combination, although some fabrics are repeated within the quilt. Barbara initially tried to limit her palette to the berry colors of red, maroon, and blue. As you can see from the finished result, she wasn't able to stick to this restriction. Some blocks were also discarded because they didn't seem to fit in with everything else. Barbara muses that it was a case of, "Good blocks, wrong quilt." A variety of lights were used in the background area. Some are suggestive of the old shirtings used in quilts from around the turn of this century.

Barbara's inspiration was an 1880 silk quilt featured in *The Quilt Engagement Calendar 1996*. The basket handle was modified as she drafted her own block. The original quilt was only five rows wide; Barbara's needed to be six. The idea of the pieced cornerstones was borrowed; the lattice/inner border and an outer border were additions. Barbara chose to work in cotton and she did include some solid-color fabrics, just as in the original. You may start with a particular quilt in mind, but the longer you work with it, the more it becomes your own.

Detail of
Scrap Basket

Helen Temple Cummins's *Scrap Basket* is a four-patch design featuring the use of diamonds. She chose to set the blocks on point and to have no sashing or plain alternate blocks. (Remember, that will make you pay more attention to the background areas in each block as you do your composing.) Perimeter triangles were necessary to square off the composition into a rectangle.

Now here's the big question: "What should the triangles contain?" Helen's inclination was to use some of the plain background fabrics in both the triangles and in a narrow one- to two-inch border, sealed with a dark binding. This solution, which she found in her quilt books, would require the least sewing. It would also probably be the most predictable and uninteresting solution.

Next, Helen sketched out her quilt to include partial blocks. (This is a comforting act for a person possessed with a strong left brain.) The drawing looked too busy to her eyes;

I loved it. In frustration, she turned back to her quilt books for guidance and inspiration. She was able to find examples among her beloved antique quilts of all the possible solutions: lighter triangles, darker triangles, and partial pieced blocks. Remember, this makes all the options "legal".

So Helen went back to her design wall. She carefully took a strip of plain muslin and laid it over an outside row of baskets so only half baskets were left exposed. This short-cut method allowed her to see quickly what partial basket blocks would look like. Much to her surprise, she loved the effect. The quilt came alive! It wasn't too busy in real life.

Often the more difficult solution is visually more exciting and satisfactory. That makes the added effort worthwhile. Don't always opt for the easy way out. The quilt will be around for a long time and you'll be glad you did the extra work.

Helen had these comments: "This was a great process for me, because I was called on to use many fabrics in the same pattern in a 'nonconsistent way.' It was only in doing it that I really saw the full scope of what it was about. I composed on a design wall, auditioning different fabrics—light, dark, busy, calm, large-scale, small-scale—until a block felt right, then the quilt as a whole felt right. I learned to trust my instincts and, when my laboring mind blocked that, I was encouraged to look at antique quilts to see what worked. The quilt was not preplanned; it unfolded gradually, block by block. I now feel that a scrap quilt should be unaffected and unsophisticated. It was a freeing experience."

Scrap Basket
58" x 73". 1997. Helen Temple Cummins, Carmichael, California. (Block pattern page 138)

Working With Only Plaids and Stripes

When selecting and composing a plaid quilt, follow the same general guidelines I have laid out for scrap quilts. In addition, you'll have to learn to see and understand the patterns that are on the directional fabrics. This chart will be helpful:

In order for a plaid/stripe fabric to show to its best advantage, it shouldn't duplicate the fabric next to it. Your eye has to be able to discern some kind of difference (refer to Chapter 2: *Plaids and Stripes*, pages 35-39). There's always the matter of color and value. That aside, pair fabrics from different parts of the calm/busy chart. Just as in regular scrap quilts, some areas of the quilt will have to be more busy, and some will have to be quiet. Whatever you do, *Don't Match*!

CALM	BUSY
ON-GRAIN	OFF-GRAIN
SYMMETRICAL	ASYMMETRICAL
EVEN PATTERN	UNEVEN PATTERN
STRIPES	PLAIDS
SOLID LINES	IKAT
LOW VALUE CONTRAST	HIGH VALUE CONTRAST
FLAT READING	INTERIOR ILLUMINATION
SMALL-SCALE	LARGE-SCALE
TWO COLORS	MULTICOLOR

Chinese Coins

The 1930s *Chinese Coins* is made from all plaids and stripes. The rectangular coins, of varying height but the same width, are all bias cut. The quilt isn't too busy because of the repetitive consistency in the grainline.

In contrast to the coins, the vertical sashing strips are cut so they are parallel (well, almost) to the edge of the quilt. The yellow bars in the gray stripe don't line up across the quilt, due to patching. This offset look adds energy and character. You can see that the plaid fabric was also patched and not cut consistently. The two fabrics used for these sashes could have been arranged in an alternating rhythm, but instead the quiltmaker chose to be more asymmetrical in her placement.

The right and left borders are obviously made from the leftovers from the rest of the quilt, as both grainlines are employed. The bottom edge of the quilt may, or may not, be considered a border. I believe that strip was added to increase the length. You will notice that the vertical sashes extend into the area, but the color changes to pink. The vertical seams don't line up perfectly, which tells me the strip was added.

The back of the quilt was pieced together with strips of pink and green sateen, typical of the era. The backing was then brought around to the front as the binding. The patching accounts for the color changes you can see. It was fun to play detective and analyze this quilt. I could almost hear the quiltmaker's mental wheels turn as she made various choices, working with what was at hand.

Chinese Coins
62" x 79". 1930. Collection of author.

Rebecca Rohrkaste was inspired by seeing the antique *Chinese Coins* at a show. She decided to make her own interpretation, which she calls *Tertiary*. Her memory was obviously most impressed by the bias cut rectangles, because she eliminated everything else. She did duplicate the use of tall and short units, but Rebecca's are consistent in size.

Rebecca's quilt is a "pared down to the essentials" version. She was surprised that the original quilt had the sashes and borders when she viewed it again at a later date. Because of the design simplicity, Rebecca was able to concentrate on her coloration. Her contemporary quilt has a wonderful luminous quality. Machine quilting was done with the "tag ends" of all her various threads.

Rebecca said, "I was immediately charmed when I saw the antique quilt. Making my own version was another way of enjoying and appreciating the original. I liked the simple graphics and I loved the scale and colors of the plaids. They reminded

Tertiary
55" x 72". 1996. Rebecca Rohrkaste, Berkeley, California.

me of kids' old plaid shirts or dresses, and aprons from the 1930s, '40s, and '50s. The unfussy, simple construction was very evocative for me and I'm left to make up my own stories about the quilt.

"I used new fabrics, vintage feed sacks, and several fabrics cut from old clothes. I also love to use simple repeating shapes in my quilts and come up with something that seems both familiar and a little unusual.

Eliminating the vertical sashing allowed for more color and value interaction between the rectangles. The quilt started looking like strata on my design wall and reminded me of some Paul Klee paintings I'd been looking at recently. The colors that worked for me turned out to be mostly the tertiaries on the color wheel." Tertiaries are colors such as: red-orange, yellow-orange, yellow-green, blue-green, etc.

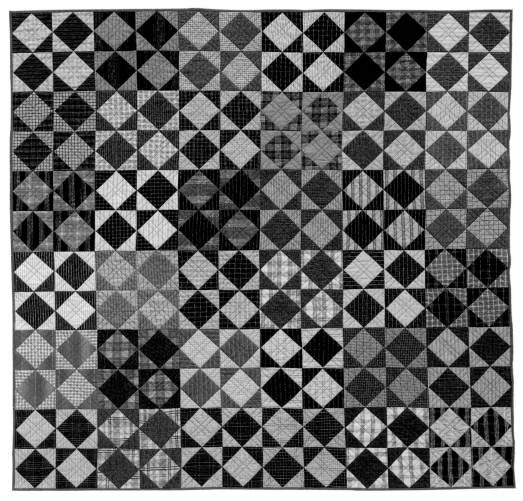

Bound for Kobe
60" x 60". 1995. Naoko Anne Ito (facilitator), Berkeley, California. Machine quilted by Rebecca Rohrkaste.

SQUARE WITHIN a SQUARE variations

Bound for Kobe uses the very simple shape of a diamond surrounded by four triangles. For this California Star, four units equal a block. You can readily see that only two fabrics are used per block. Because no plain blocks or sashing was used, some of you will see a secondary pattern of stars (you have to ignore the colors and look only at the seamlines).

Following the disastrous earthquake in Kobe, Japan, *Patchwork Tsushin* magazine requested that quilts be made for a relief fund to benefit the survivors. Naoko Anne Ito organized a group to make a quilt from my area. I donated the plaids and stripes from some of those I had styled. Many of the blue and black fabrics were inspired by antique Japanese textiles.

Notice that different values and hues of blue are used. The addition of black merely gets the quilt to maximum dark. It's still a blue quilt. On purpose, a variety of lights were used, all the way from pure whites to dark beiges. I selected pairs of fabric to be joined. After the blocks were sewn, I arranged them on my design wall to keep the eye moving. The large-scale plaids were included to give some visual excitement.

Many of the sewers had been to Japan. We were pleased that the quilt felt Japanese to us. There was a beautiful simplicity and serenity to it. (Several of the team exactly duplicated the quilt for themselves). Besides basic machine quilting in the seams, stitching with red Sulky® rayon was diagonally laid over the quilt in double lines. The quilt was also bound in red. This was to represent the loss of life in that disaster symbolically.

Plaid Opus #1 by Caroline Weber-Pyne started out as a five-patch (five-unit grid) called Mrs. Keller's Nine Patch. As Caroline began composing, she unknowingly changed the value placement from the two-value block given in the book, to a three-value block using three, four, or five fabrics. Caroline discovered that when she placed the block on point, she could create a secondary pattern. The middle units of the five-patch block join visually value-wise to create a false diagonal sashing. This in turn surrounds a Square Within a Square. If you look closely at the repetition of color within one block, you can see the true layout of the quilt.

Original two-value block.

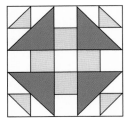

New three-value block.

Half-blocks were used to fill in the perimeter triangles. Caroline simplified the half-block by substituting a large square or a large triangle for the division used in the interior blocks in the rest of the quilt.

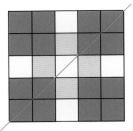

Simplification of block for perimeter triangles.

Caroline describes the design process: "I had never worked with plaids, except as an accent in a quilt. Using one plaid was not difficult; using many plaids and stripes together I found daunting. I found that I could only work on the piece a couple of hours at a time, without ending up with a headache."

Caroline has an astigmatism (an irregularity of the eye lens so light rays from an object do not meet in a single point, resulting in an indistinct or distorted image). This may account for the headache, as plaids are more busy viewed on point. She might also have been thinking too hard as she searched for the secondary pattern on her new design wall.

Suggestion: If plaids seem to bother your eyes, work with blocks that are placed parallel to the edge of the quilt. Also, don't worry about secondary patterns, which would require more serious looking with your eyes.

Caroline continues, "It was okay to let go of my control and let the fabrics work with and for themselves. By the time it came to piecing the border, I had surrendered completely to the fabrics, and let them take over. The border was the easiest to do. Taking Roberta's teachings to heart, the backing was pieced from all the leftovers. The binding took the project just one step further, using the cuttings from the backing and some leftover plaid binding I had from another quilt. I quilted the border letting the lines of the fabrics speak to me and dictate the design. I used a washable wool batting which made the hand quilting experience even that much better.

"The overall result pleased me more than I had expected and it has turned into my favorite quilt so far. I plan to do more with plaids, in different patterns. I am looking forward to the challenges each new quilt will present to me."

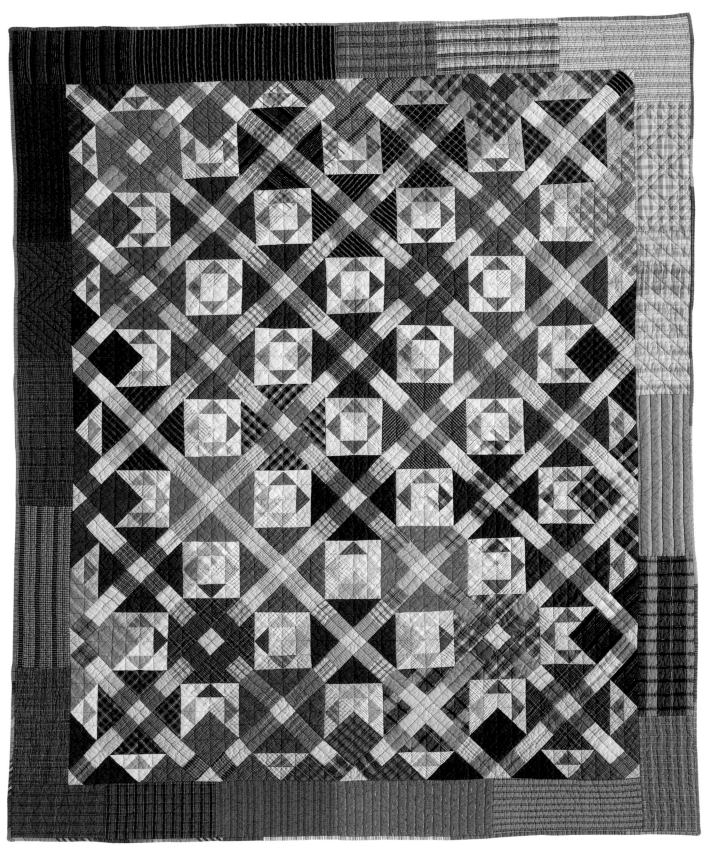

Plaid Opus #1
64" x 82". 1996. Caroline Weber-Pyne, Oxnard, California.

Vicki Johnson challenged herself to use two blocks she likes in her quilt. *Saturday and Meetings Blue Plaid* quilt uses only plaids and stripes I designed. Angles and Squares blocks became the body of the quilt. Squares in Squares blocks were used for the border. Both patterns were set on point.

The quilt was initially limited to light blues. Vicki thought turquoise or green-blue would serve as a spark, but this proved too dull. Darker blue blocks were added to the composition on the design wall. At some point, Vicki became confused and decided to turn to her recently purchased computer. In Aldus SuperPaint® she drew the blocks in outline. This allowed her to fine-tune the arrangement and size. Then she copied the outline drawing and tried different "paints" to play with the values. This was how she came up with the beautiful arrangement of her lights and darks.

Saturday and Meetings Blue Plaid Quilt
63" x 90". 1993. Vicki L. Johnson, Soquel, California. (Block patterns pages 135, 136)

Now it was time to go back to the real fabric. Vicki made enough blocks for the whole top. Something was still wrong— she needed a more contrasting spark. Lavender did the job!

Vicki decided the handwoven fabrics needed to be hand quilted to retain the soft feel of the quilt. She says, "Since this quilt was for me, and not one of my art quilts which I sell, I did it in my free time. Saturday, which we have set aside as a no-work day, and meetings, at which I usually don't have any handwork to do, were my free time. I have been pleased at the response and interest this quilt has been given, since it is different from most of my work."

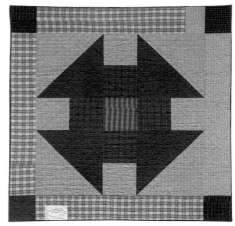

She Did The Best She Could II by Nadi Lane was made using another very similar five-patch block (five-unit grid) called Churn Dash. Anywhere from two to four fabrics are used per block, which gives a fair number of possible variations. Nadi does regret the position of the center block, which reads as a cross, because it draws too much attention to that spot. Only plaids and stripes were used. Nadi cut the plaid fabrics on-grain, diagonally, and casually off-grain.

The blocks are placed diagonally to the edge and are divided with light sashing strips. Darker cornerstones made from leftovers were added at the intersections. Perimeter triangles cut from five different medium plaids have been randomly positioned around the outside. As no official border was used, a collage of dark plaids in the binding defines the outside edge.

Originally, Nadi planned to sew the blocks directly to each other. Then she started thinking about all the seam allowances coming together, so she opted for the sashes. She said, "My solution was more pragmatic than artistic." Many quiltmakers from yesteryear also made that choice, maybe for the same reason. Remember, from a visual standpoint, sashes allow you to combine unruly blocks more easily.

She Did the Best She Could II
65" x 65". 1991. Nadi Lane, Agoura, California.

Nadi did the quilting in five days. She said, "I used the 'Hurry-up-winter-is-coming School of Quilting.'" The two-inch diagonal square grid was purposely quilted with larger quilting stitches than her normal size. This was to reinforce the country or utilitarian look of the quilt. The quilt back is one giant Churn Dash.

Back of *She Did the Best She Could II.*
(Block pattern page 137)

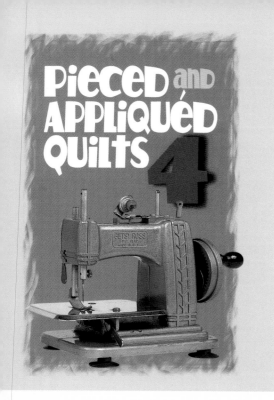

PiECED AND APPLIQUÉD QUILTS 4

This Old Portland House by Barbara Dallas uses a traditional pieced house block pattern, a favorite of Barbara's. It was made to honor her purchase and subsequent renovation of an old house.

When Barbara began she planned to make a green quilt. To her surprise, it soon proved to be boring. Barbara found she had to go all the way from yellow-green to green to blue-green to create the interest she was looking for. Notice that there's also a range in value, scale, and type of fabric patterns used. Taken individually, any individual house isn't necessarily beautiful. The quilt is successful because of the total look of the fabrics, not because of any one combination. There's less risk of failure when you work with many fabrics. In this scrap quilt some fabrics are repeated, but no houses match each other.

Notice that the quilt is not built in a traditional checkerboard format. Instead, it's assembled in strips so the house blocks are offset. The plain alternate blocks are really rectangles. Leaves and wonderful carpenter tools float across the surface of the quilt, sometimes overlapping into a house block.

The leaves are repeated around the border in a whirlwind fashion. A beautiful selection of commercial fabrics was chosen to depict the realistic leaves. Barbara was witnessing her first dramatic fall color change as she was working on the quilt, and it made a strong impression on her. At the fabric store she selected fabrics that duplicated what she was seeing. The stems were accomplished by using a narrow machine satin stitch. The vein lines were added as quilting stitches.

A dogtooth border frames the leaves on both sides. Barbara was inspired by seeing this appliqué border treatment used in some Baltimore Album quilts. Much planning went into the execution so that the corners were resolved correctly. Barbara didn't want the distraction of a separate binding, so she faced the outside edge with a strip of the backing fabric which was then turned to the back side.

As quiltmakers become more proficient in their skills, it's common to see both piecing and appliqué within one quilt. Some shapes can be depicted using either technique, but others can't. It boils down to the simple fact that it's just easier to piece some shapes and to appliqué others. Not knowing how to do both techniques seriously limits what you can do. (Refer to Chapter 6, Skills, for help.) Let's look at some quilts that combine both techniques.

This Old Portland House
59" x 69". 1996. Barbara Dallas, Portland, Oregon.

My aunt Elsie Peterson once told me an enchanting true story which led me to make a quilt. This is the tale she recounted: "It was way back when I was in high school. I came home one day and my mother had the dining room table covered with baskets of dishes and sheet cakes. She was cutting heart-shaped cakes to ice and decorate for two book clubs she was having together. We called them the 'Up the Road Book Club' and the 'Down the Road Book Club.'

"I was eager to help, so I began cutting cakes. Guess I got tired, so I leaned too heavily on the table, and over it went, with cakes, dishes borrowed from my aunt, and me! Naturally, my mother was very upset and gave me a tongue lashing I'll never forget! I'll always remember that the good part for me was that my dad came in then and said, 'Oh, Mama don't fuss. You know she didn't mean to do it.'"

This touching childhood recollection became *Aunt Elsie's Broken Dishes*. A simple sketch roughly drawn on the back of an advertising circular became the basis for this quilt. Notice that the sketch isn't a complete rendering of the finished quilt, but merely a suggestion of some possible shapes that might be used.

Appropriate fabric selection would do half the work for me in translating this story. I found fabrics with "tablecloth" and "china" patterns on them. I eventually decided on a skewed format to help suggest movement. The borders were composed of Broken Dishes blocks rendered in two sizes to keep the feeling of things being helter-skelter.

A surviving dish that recently broke

Because the fabrics were so suggestive to me, the quilting designs followed easily. The two pinks used for the background (tablecloth) were a sateen woven in a checkerboard—thus the quilted grid. The silverware was floated across this surface to add more visual interest. Water was stitched spewing from the teapot. The design I had casually doodled on the plate in the original sketch, as well as the silverware and water

quilting designs present in the drawing, appear as quilting stitches in the finished quilt.

Aunt Elsie's Broken Dishes isn't a true scrap quilt because it was composed using a limited number of fabrics. However, because large-scale patterns were selected, there's a visual scrap-like inconsistency in coloration in the Broken Dishes blocks. This is due to the small size of the templates in relation to the large size of the fabric design. A better glimpse of the pattern of the fabrics intact can be seen in the teapot and plates.

The right fabrics just seemed to present themselves for this quilt. My Aunt Elsie favored pink in her home decor. Believe it or not, the fabrics that initiated the quilt were the two shades of pink sateen which looked like a tablecloth to me. Because of an initial good fabric selection, one insight followed another until the quilt was finished.

Original sketch

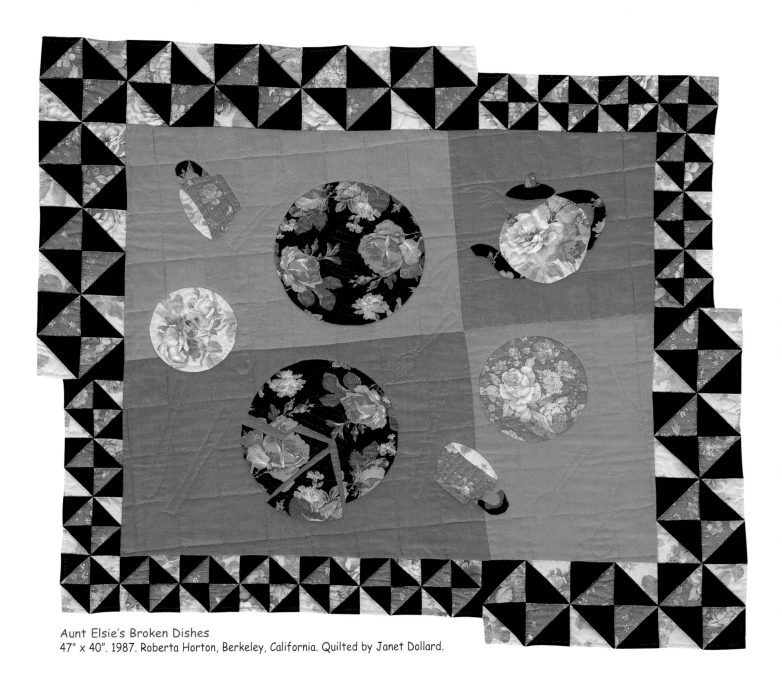

Aunt Elsie's Broken Dishes
47" x 40". 1987. Roberta Horton, Berkeley, California. Quilted by Janet Dollard.

Ode to My Featherweight is a salute to all the Singer Featherweights™ in my life. On my mother's machine I learned to sew doll clothes; later, my own clothing. As a quiltmaker I bought one I use to this day for my piecing. The name tag on the machine in the quilt belonged to my grandmother, who pieced her quilts on a Featherweight. I own that machine now, too: sturdy, dependable, and lightweight; a comfortable friend which sews merely forward and backward in an endless straight seam.

At various times I doodled some images I might include in a quilt. As you can see, the quilt looks like neither, but has elements from both.

The actual quilt wasn't worked out on graph paper first. Starting with the center rectangle, each stage was made using my quilter's ruler, cutting as I went along. I used whole-inch increments (no fractions). I had to remember to add on seam allowance to each piece. I didn't want a square center, so I added the pincushion (which is like my grandmother's) and the scissors to fill up the rectangle. Once I freehand paper-cut the sewing machine, the size of the center rectangle was determined. I satin stitched the elements in the center rectangle before going on to the next step.

Since I had light-colored backgrounds for my center panel and second border, I decided to separate the two with a narrow medium-colored first border. This area later became a place to sew vintage buttons given to me by a dear friend. The lengths for this border were random-cut with an attempt not to have seams line up across the quilt.

The letters in the second border are a summation of the quilting process. I decided to use light-colored plaids and stripes for the backgrounds. When the lettering was cut, I found I didn't need the cornerstones I had included in the first drawing. The lengths of the background strips needed for the letters were calculated by dividing the border length measurement by the number of characters. Each word was stitched to the background before the blocks were joined to form the border.

Both drawings had featured an outer border. Theoretically, I did want this, but physically I didn't feel like expending the effort, so the quilt got put aside for awhile. One day I remembered a stack of Log Cabin blocks given to me by Harriet Stull during the 1970s when I taught in Adult Education. Harriet only made full-size quilts and evidently she had decided she didn't want to do the requisite number to complete the project. When I located the blocks I saw they were made with old familiar fabric friends from that early period of my quilting career. I know Harriet would be pleased that I finally put her blocks to good use.

Sketch #1

Sketch #2

Ode to My Featherweight
43" x 27". 1996. Roberta Horton, Berkeley, California. Quilted by Janet Dollard.

I decided to look for other vintage blocks in my stash. I found three more sets. The brown Broken Dishes blocks across the bottom are from the 1890s. The blue Nine Patches replicate some from the 1930s that were too fragile to include. The grouping in the upper right-hand corner with the feeling of 1910 also had to be re-created.

You will see that it was necessary to add a "coping wedge" in the top row to achieve the needed length. Many fabrics were auditioned before I found the one that wouldn't be too noticeable.

By the way, the quilt backing is a fabric that features paper dolls, a favorite childhood pastime for me.

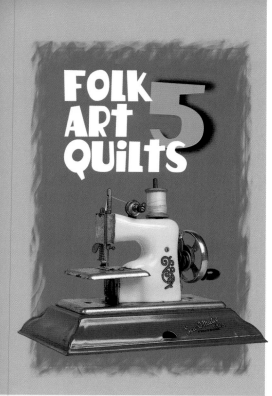

FOLK ART QUILTS 5

I have long collected what I consider to be folk art. But what is it really? The technical definition has seemed to broaden in recent years, or at least it has been subdivided into categories, like self-taught, naive, visionary, outsider art, etc. The word primitive is often associated with folk art.

WHAT IS FOLK ART?

I'm particularly fond of the folk art paintings of colonial America—they make my heart sing. They were created by itinerant painters who weren't formally trained. Body proportion isn't always accurate—you see this particularly in the arms and hands of the figures. Folk art styles also appeared in many other mediums, such as wood, pottery, metal, and even fabric. Some people consider all quilts to be folk art, but I don't. Some quilts are too precise and too well proportioned to be called naive and primitive.

Many of you are familiar with Grandma Moses and her depictions of times past in New England. Clementine Hunter depicted Southern plantation life. Both of these women are considered folk artists. A more recent time period in which lots of folk art was produced was during the hippie era of the 1970s. People were encouraged to express themselves artistically, to "do their own thing." Think of all the hand-decorated and embroidered clothes and the ubiquitous painted Volkswagen™ bus. For a short while, everyone could be an artist.

For my purposes in this quilt book, I define folk art simply as art done by us folk. It means that commercial patterns aren't used. It's your own art style, for better or worse. The quilt happens as spontaneously as possible. Here are some of your options when making a folk art-style quilt:

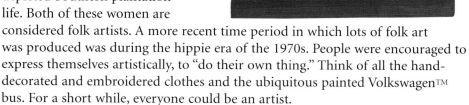

Tramp art

Cat by Mr. Finn

Bird house?

1. Proportions don't have to be accurate.

2. Whatever is most important can be portrayed as bigger; less important things can be made small, or eliminated.

3. Depth perception can be eliminated by using a head-on view. The finished subject will look 2-D rather than 3-D.

4. Items can float rather than be grounded.

5. Sewing techniques don't have to be of heirloom quality.

Select methods that give a primitive feeling. Large stitches in appliqué and quilting can be used. This is a perfect project to experiment with new techniques—and leave in the errors. Nancy Freeman has used different hand stitching styles in her quilt *Three Birds, Two Fish, and a Pot of Flowers* on page 109.

The hardest part for those who don't consider themselves natural-born artists is learning to accept that your own art style is okay. To do so, we must learn to accept our own uniqueness and individuality. Pause for just a minute and look at your writing hand. Inspect the wrinkle lines, bumps, lumps, calluses, and scars. The more your hand is used, the more story it has to tell. Now compare this hand with your non-writing hand. You may notice that it's more refined than your working hand. There are fewer marks on it; the fingers may even be smaller.

If you can find another individual to compare hands with, you will really see some differences. One person may have bigger hands, or longer fingers. Fingernails are shaped differently. Very few people have the beautiful hands featured in advertising or in the movies. Hand models don't use their hands for everyday tasks because their hands represent their income. Quilters have working hands.

Just as hands vary, so do individual art styles. Who is to say that one person's

Detail of *Three Birds, Two Fish, and a Pot of Flowers*. For full quilt see page 109.

style is better than another's? Tastes in the art world change. Art movements come and go. Your written signature is a personal art style. It will change over a lifetime. Remember your first efforts as a small child to print your own name. Then you learned cursive writing. Perhaps as a teenager you made little circles or hearts for the dot of the letter i. Eventually your writing style stabilized into its present recognizable form. As you age, it may change again due to arthritis and diminishing eyesight.

People often become folk artists when they retire. First of all, they have more time to do the things they've always wanted to do. With age also comes confidence. We know who we are. At some point folk artists cease worrying about what others think. There's an honesty to folk art. The maker is saying, "Here it is, like it or lump it."

Quiltmaking lends itself readily to a folk art style. The more primitive your efforts, the better the results. All the quilts in this chapter were composed on a design wall. Remember, having everything on one visual plane allows you to critique your work more easily. The ultimate goal in folk art quilts is to be able to cut your own original patterns, hopefully directly into the fabric. Don't say you can't do either of these things until you read Chapter 6: Skills (page 119-133). For now, forget about the nitty-gritty, how-to details, and enjoy the quilts.

Underneath view of hat brim. Folk art is often signed.

Wood head from Indiana

FROM INSPIRATION TO ORIGINAL QUILT

The following quilts are examples of people creating their own original designs. Many cut directly into the fabric; some initially cut paper patterns. I will first discuss three folk art quilts in depth. Then I will talk about some categories of subject matter that work well in a folk art style. All contain simple shapes. The selection of a familiar topic is the easiest entry into doing your own original work.

Frau Horton,
Frau Horton

People often ask me how long it takes me to make a quilt. *Frau Horton, Frau Horton* (page 98) is the culmination of a quilt I have tried to make since I first visited Germany in 1992. That is, it took five years from first thought to finished quilt. The final version is folk art, and in this case, it was inspired by real folk art. I returned twice more to teach in Braunfels, a romantic town with a castle at the top of the hill. Each time I collected ideas, took photographs, made visits to folk museums, and saw old towns. I couldn't put my finger on what exactly I wanted to do. Meanwhile, I dutifully collected authentic German fabrics and ribbons, just in case inspiration should hit.

On my first visit my hostess had introduced me to Monika Mosburger, a dollmaker who also collects and sells old folk costumes. Her dolls were clothed in the appropriate attire for Marburg and the neighboring villages. I dreamed about those dolls for two years and went to see Monika again the next time I visited Germany.

Inspiration: photos and postcards. Photos by Monika Mosburger.

(I had a case of serious coveting, but the dolls were no longer for sale.) Twice at the teaching seminar different groups came wearing their traditional folk costumes. I had been fascinated. I guess the closest Americans have come to producing a national folk costume would be a pair of Levi's® jeans, a cowboy hat, and boots.

Then one day after my second visit, I received an envelope filled with pictures. These photos were my consolation prize for not being able to buy a doll. The images triggered my imagination. I could piece some figures wearing the traditional fabrics and ribbons. I decided I wanted to try free-form piecing. (Refer to Creative Piecing: Free-form, page 130, to see how the shapes were created.)

All the fabric in the quilt, except the faces, legs, and background, is German. The fabric reminds me of the small-print calicoes used when I first started making quilts in the 1970s. There were also traditional stripes and plaids. My dancing women are generic; that is, they aren't faithful depictions of garments worn in a specific village. I didn't have enough knowledge to undertake that challenge. Each figure has on a vest, sometimes made from ribbon, and an apron. I completed the central portion of the quilt, then sat around waiting for the next idea as I worked on other quilt projects.

The next inspiration for the project came during my third trip, in 1996. I was taken to see Freilichtmuseum Hessenpark, an outdoor collection of buildings that had been moved from villages in the Hessen area so that they could be preserved and not lost.

The decorations on the buildings were from an earlier period than the Victorian romantic idealization of Braunfels. The designs look, at first glance, to be symmetrical, but they really aren't (study the photos carefully). I found this wonderfully exciting! These designs were truly hand done!

I decided I could adapt these ideas for a top and bottom border. I consciously decided not to fold my paper in half when I paper cut my shapes. I also tried to make some shapes bigger than their matching partner on the other side. (See Design Source for Paper Cutting, page 123.)

Initially the border was composed of German fabrics I hadn't gotten around to using in the project. The colors happened to be different from the blues and blacks used in the interior. There was a peachy orange, two different patterns in the same color of magenta, a light turquoise-green, and a very dark green. The orange, one of the magentas, and the dark green unfortunately repeated the same motif. The borders didn't match the rest of the quilt, but they matched each other. The coloration was a little startling in contrast to the rest of the quilt, and I wondered if anyone but me would think they belonged together. I did have the necessary repetition to pull things together, but was it enough?

Another problem with the borders was that they didn't look as scrappy as the rest of the quilt. I had tried to cut the fabric in different ways, if the motif allowed, and tried not to be too repetitive in the fabric placement, but these changes weren't enough. I found that I had to add

Freilichtmuseum Hessenpark.
Photo by Roberta Horton.

Photos by
Roberta Horton.

two more dark blue fabrics I had previously rejected. I also found a small fragment of light blue from the central area that could be substituted for the turquoise in several places. The color and pattern of the fabrics needed to be mixed up a little bit more to impart the appropriate personality. The addition of the navy blue also tied the borders into the center area.

I hand appliquéd the borders, because I consider this quilt a serious

effort. I didn't use the popular freezer paper technique because I wanted irregularities to develop as I sewed. An inner border of ribbons was stitched onto the quilt after the hand quilting was completed. The ribbons came in several widths and lengths, which necessitated the solution as seen—another example of making do. I feel that the ribbon inner border brings the colors of the different areas of the quilt together.

Frau Horton, Frau Horton
44" x 54". 1997. Roberta Horton, Berkeley, California. Quilted by Janet Dollard.

Quilts "Я" Us
53" x 42". 1995. Tracy Allen, Pacheco, California.

 Quilts " Я " Us

Quilts "Я" Us was created by Tracy Allen in one of my folk art classes. I began by having everyone cut their name in paper (see Letters, page 120). Next, Tracy collaged a background of several different plaids and stripes. Moving ahead, she paper cut an amorphous shape she saw on a note card. Two of these shapes were then cut in fabric and added to the composition. The quilt seemed to be taking shape rapidly.

Tracy stated she wanted to feature hands on her quilt. I can still hear her say, "I have a wonderful hand pattern at home that I'll bring tomorrow." I was stunned, as were the rest of the class members! We indignantly volunteered our own hands as patterns. Notice how each hand shape is different, and therefore unique. Tracy was then inspired to select fabric that made a statement about the donors' fabric or color preference.

Tracy collects antique quilt blocks and decided to add some in the border. She filled in with some random plaids and added buttons from her grandmother's button box. Tracy concluded, "I have been curious about the hearts and hands often found in antique quilts and wondered if they came about in the same manner as mine? My thoughts transferred to fabric—what an accomplishment. What would the antique buttons and blocks say if they could talk?"

Sundogs Over Susitna
45" x 49". 1997. Monica Jenicek Lyall, Chugiak, Alaska. Collection of Clay Borden, Becky Watson, and Wiley Borden.

 Sundogs over Susitna

Sundogs over Susitna is by Monica Jenicek Lyall. Monica recalls, "I modified a panel of Nancy Crow fabric to provide the background and the ice of Cook Inlet. Then I added the view from my living room window of Mount Susitna and the Alaska Range as the sun is setting (which is how it looked to me when I came home from Roberta's class at the end of the first day). The dogs then just fell into place."

About a week later Monica's close friend announced she was pregnant. *Sundogs Over Susitna* was now to be a baby quilt. The expectant mother is seriously interested in dog obedience training. This gave Monica ideas for the machine quilting. Words like woof, bark, howl, sit, and stay could be subtly stitched. The bottom border reads, "Good dog, exercise finished. Okay!" Dog obedience aficionados will recognize "Exercise finished" as the command at the end of an obedience training exercise. "Okay" releases the dog from whatever task he or she is performing.

Notice how Monica has framed her quilt. The left and top border are the same width; the right and bottom borders are narrower. For the most part, the border fabrics are slightly darker than the interior adjoining area. The black mountain range fabric extends into the border. One dog also floats over that border. It was necessary to give that dog a halo of contrasting fabrics to make it show up on the base fabric. Monica has created her own polka dots for the dog on the right.

The label on the back of the quilt is Monica's first attempt at free-form piecing (see Creative Piecing Skills: Free-form page 130.)

A Single House

When you work in a folk art style, work with things that are familiar to you. A house is a good starting place. It's one of the first subjects children draw. Few of us live in a picturesque log cabin or a quaint cottage, and no one I know lives in a house that looks exactly like Barbara Dallas's pieced house block on page 89. Yet we know what Barbara's generic shape represents.

 Sylvia's Quilt Studio

Sylvia's Quilt Studio is Sylvia Richen's fantasy. Don't we all wish we had somewhere to retreat from our hectic daily lives; someplace to do nothing but indulge in our quilting urges? A fantasy has the advantage that you don't have to be able to do an architectural rendering of a real location. Sometimes you can get too hung up on making realistic details which can then inhibit you from getting started making the quilt.

Sylvia's quilt is done in a folksy primitive style. Therefore, her flowers are joyous and bold. Real flowers wouldn't be in such a large scale in relation to the house—that's the advantage of folk art. Sylvia has also created three different tree shapes for more variety in the composition.

Sylvia's Quilt Studio
50" x 56". 1997. Sylvia Richen, Portland, Oregon.

Log Cabin blocks create a nice border. Notice that the yellow centers vary in both fabric and dimension. Log width also varies. The blocks aren't composed in the traditional light/dark division. In other words, the Log Cabin blocks were individually crafted.

Sylvia had this to say about the process: "As a quilter this was a challenge because I had only done structured, color-coordinated quilts. When Roberta took my ruler away and said, 'Cut' I froze. She then encouraged me to just start by cutting my name out of fabric (see Letters, pages 119-120). From there on things just seemed to go together. I am very pleased with the results. By completing this quilt I have been given a freedom in my quilting I haven't had before in working with scraps and colors."

Pete's Place

Pete's Place was made for my dad's 90th birthday. He does, in fact, live in a quaint cottage, situated behind my house. It's nestled in my garden, which is filled with flowers, birds, and visiting cats. The cats in the piece are generic—a grey and white tropical leaf print produced the best looking stripes. I opted to work with floral prints rather than creating my own flowers. (My unattainable goal is to keep everything blooming in Technicolor® year round.)

The birdbath, rose trellis, and arbor do exist. There's a partial fence. The new replacement tree will someday be as big as the one in the quilt. Things I eliminated were: all my dad's wind chimes, the battery-operated croaking frog that announces visitors, and the structural trellis that holds up the roses on the front of the cottage. I selected the sky fabric to denote all the unusual colorations against which I have seen his cottage silhouetted.

I have always loved the lettering found on old quilts. I decided to piece the title of the quilt in big bold letters reminiscent of a movie marquee. My dad was trained as an engineer, and I thought this controlled style would appeal to him. (Directions for doing this can be found in Letters, pages 119-120.)

This quilt combines many methods of appliqué. Most areas are machine satin stitched in matching colors. I used raw-edge appliqué for all the flowers. Some pesky areas, like the dragonfly, are hand stitched. In other words, I did what seemed easiest, or in some cases, whatever took the least time.

Pete's cottage. Photo by Roberta Horton.

Pete's Place
52" x 43". 1997. Roberta Horton, Berkeley, California. Quilted by Janet Dollard.

Home

Kathy Ezell decided to create her own home in fabric. The contemporary house is in a typical Pacific Northwest setting—lots of trees. The drawback was that there's a big driveway, and a large percentage of what you see from the street is the garage door. One option open to Kathy was to do a photo-realistic image; another was to do an architectural rendering, more like a blueprint. Or, Kathy could try for a more folk art style.

Kathy decided to take the folk art route, the advantage being that you can eliminate unimportant things—which she did. Kathy cropped her image for *Home* to capture just the essence of her house. Basically she featured the welcoming entryway and added lots of trees and flowers. Don't we wish our flowers grew as lush as Kathy's!

Kathy had this to say: "Rendering my home in fabric from memory was entertaining. Not having to make an accurate representation of the house and landscape, only the expression of it, was very liberating. I could have a red door instead of a green one, my rhododendron trusses could be as big as cars. Trees were cut freehand from plaids or prints and could be any size I wanted. It's quite surprising how simple it is to do. Working in the folk art style, not being concerned with fitting blocks, matching seams, or turning under edges, was joyous and fun."

Home
27" x 27". 1996. Kathy Ezell, Mukilteo, Washington.

The Ezell home. Photo by Kathy Ezell.

Places

One building can grow into a cluster of houses or a village. The resulting quilt just becomes more complicated and complex. For the quilter, more thinking, planning, and stewing will be required.

 Homes, Sweet Homes

Maggie Kolvenbach decided to make a wall quilt entitled *Homes, Sweet Homes* for her daughter. Laura loves plaids, so Maggie made sure to include many in the composition. Check out the variety of grainlines employed. When a plaid was used twice in a building, Maggie changed the direction the second time so that the fabric would look different. A wide bias binding of plaid frames the composition.

Some special buildings were included. The yellow schoolhouse near the center of the quilt denotes Laura's profession. The roof fabric, appropriately enough, has letters printed on it. Maggie's own home is to the right, just above the schoolhouse (look for the red chimney). To the direct right is the home of the Swedish watercolorist Carl Larsson, who specialized in pictures of family life. Larsson is Maggie's favorite artist, so she felt he should reside in her community.

The church, borrowed from New Hampshire, has tie-dyed fabric for the windows. A friend of Maggie's son was married there. The blue house, front and center, is another daughter's home. Can you identify any other famous homes?

The sky is strip pieced from an assortment of similar blue fabrics. Notice how Maggie has used the stripe and plaid on the bias to give more contrast, and therefore energy, among the other blues. This area is then overlaid with round clouds. Maggie also decided to have round and oval shaped trees. Both of these choices give a folk art feeling to the piece.

Homes, Sweet Homes
36" x 26". 1995. Maggie Kolvenbach, Mt. Kisco, New York. Collection of Laura Kolvenbach, Houston, Texas.

Garage with House
Attached
53" x 48". 1997. Valerie
Boode, Red Deer, Alberta,
Canada.

 **Garage with
House Attached**

Garage with House Attached by
Valerie Boode encapsulates all the
places she has lived into one quilt.
Starting with the farmhouse of her
youth in the upper left, she then
added depictions of the residences
she has lived in with her husband
and two sons. Also included are her
husband's cherished vehicles, each
with the make and year done in
machine quilting (e.g., '34 Chev).
Valerie, her husband, and sons are
also rendered in fabric. The quilt will
become a pictorial record when the
oral record is forgotten.

Valerie stated, "I learned a lot during
both the design and construction of
this quilt. To be asked to quickly cut
directly into the fabric was a loose
and creative process for me. I cut
from my mind's eye on a familiar
topic where my memory dictated the
design rather than a photograph. The
result proved to be a delightful trip
down memory lane.

"The idea came to me for this quilt as
I was walking back to my residence
hall to get my sewing machine. Our
seminar was taught on a college campus in a park-like setting. I could re-
create in a folk-like manner the various homes in which I'd lived. Then as
the design evolved, I began to think
of the importance of our society's

attached garage which was evident in
each of my homes. It reminded me
of the family joke that as long as the
garage met with approval, the home
was worthy of purchase as a residence. That sentiment became the
title of the quilt."

Valerie used raw-edge appliqué and
machine quilting. Having been
through the whole design and sewing
process now, she thinks that next
time she will add the recommended
second line of stitching around the
shapes as she does her machine
quilting. The buttons were added to
emphasize the garages and to help
with the quilting.

San Miguel de Allende

San Miguel de Allende by Helen Temple Cummins represents that picturesque town in Mexico. Find Helen's house in the center of the top row. The rest of the dwellings are simply to impart her impressions of the things she sees when she is there: common color schemes and architectural details such as molding trims, grillwork, and a rose window (note the special fabrics chosen for these items). All this information could be conveyed through the use of rectangles and strips of fabric.

The village scene then became a backdrop for the large flowers, fanciful birds, and mystical animal. Helen initially planned to use these Mexican embroideries as inspiration for her own fabric appliqués. Then, at some point, she decided it would be more fun to use the real textiles. (The biggest challenge proved to be separating the nearly overlapping embroidered figures from their original muslin panel.) With the various machine techniques she tried, Helen found that the presser foot seemed to catch in the long embroidery stitches, so the shapes had to be hand appliquéd onto the quilt top.

Two different handwoven Mexican textiles from Helen's collection were used for the side borders. Notice how the shapes float over these boundaries. The airborne bird is a nice device to move your eye to the top of the scene.

The quilt is beautifully hand quilted. The texture of the adobe walls is suggested by different patterns on each house. A cobblestone-like design is quilted under the birds' feet. Some of the curved lines are done with larger stitches in six strands of embroidery floss.

Helen said, "My latest interest is Mexico. I spend a lot of time there and I'm fascinated by what I see. I'm aware of the influence of the Indians and the influence of the Spanish and wanted my piece to reflect the richness of each culture as I have observed them in San Miguel de Allende, the community I visit. This old colonial town has wonderful, well-preserved Spanish architecture. The folk art of the Indians is also very evident. In my piece I have combined the two, even using the actual embroidery of the Otomi men. It is my open-hearted expression of what I have experienced there.

"It was a delight to have Roberta remind us that folk art means 'by us.' We had to use our own patterns. She encouraged us to explore what our own expression would be. My desire in quilting is to do my thing, not someone else's."

San Miguel de Allende
54" x 46". 1997. Helen Temple Cummins, Carmichael, California.

Memories of Creeky
Springs Ranch
37" x 41". 1997.
Barbara Miller, Shingle
Springs, California.

 Memories of
Creeky Springs Ranch

Memories of Creeky Springs Ranch by
Barbara Miller captures forty years of
happy memories. The eighteen-acre
parcel with a house, outbuildings,
oak trees, and a creek, went through
escrow while she and her husband
were on their honeymoon. Her mom
warned, "Over five acres in California
is a ranch. It is not big enough to
make a living on, but sure can work
you to death."

"It proved to be a wonderful place to
raise four children and they all love

it. Each child raised animals in 4-H,
plus got involved in every other project known to man. Countless animals were memorable, like Maria the
donkey, Cactus Pete the red cat, and
Purina (Purr), the grey one. The big
dog in the corner is Miller's High
Life. Many sheep appeared over the
years, with few being memorable.
The exception was Sarah, the little
one made from the flower print. She
thought she was a person."

The quilt is a sampler of appliqué
techniques, both hand and machine.
The lettering in the border is attached

with embroidery floss in satin and
whip stitch for a nice texture. The
quilting was done by machine. The
beige background captures the color
of California in the summer, when it
doesn't rain—one of the reasons
we're called the "Golden State."

Barbara says, "I have fallen in love
with my quilt, so I will hang it in my
little house. The whole thing is my
doing, so you can't blame anyone
else. It was a lot of fun and I learned
so much from it. I still have more
to learn."

BOUQUetS

Three Birds, Two Fish,
and a Pot of Flowers
36" x 42". 1996. Nancy
Freeman, Benicia, California.

Nancy may have used many fabrics,
but she has also employed a lot of
repetition which helps to pull the
design together. A flower has the
same stem and leaves when it
appears again.

Nancy's background fabric is dark,
so the borders are light. Notice that
some flowers overlap into these
border areas, adding to the playful
spirit. The large-scale floral used in
the right and left borders is a very
formal toile-like composition and
plays against the folk mood set by the
other fabrics. Three maroon corner
blocks and a maroon binding serve
to frame the piece by reintroducing
dark to the quilt. Notice that the
lower right corner tends to fade away
so that the resolution isn't perfect.
The upper right corner block is
larger, which counterbalances this.

 **Three Birds, Two Fish,
and A Pot of Flowers**

Nancy Freeman's *Three Birds, Two
Fish, and A Pot of Flowers* has a
primitive folk art feeling. Nancy is
an experienced artist specializing
in machine satin-stitch appliqué
pictures (See *Dots* on page 42). This
is Nancy's first quilt. She used this
piece to experiment with different
ways to accomplish appliqué: both
hidden and running hand stitches,
zigzag, satin, top, and raw edge by
machine. Embroidery floss was
added for more dimension.

Nancy has used a wide range of fabrics in her quilt. Geometric fabrics
featuring dots or triangles contrast
nicely with small-scale traditional
flower prints. A printed checkerboard and a variety of stripes and
plaids provide a linear contrast to the
spotty quality of the other fabrics.
Nancy cut and sewed the printed
flowers from one fabric. This print
was used four times, each time
paired with a stem from the same
stripe fabric. In fact, you will see that

Flowers from My Garden
35" x 45". 1996. Nancy Friesen, Canby, Oregon.

 ### Flowers from My Garden

Flowers from My Garden by Nancy Friesen also has a folk art feeling because she cut her own bouquet. Each flower has its own unique shape. Stems in appliqué florals often are depicted using bias strips. Nancy's freehand-cut stems are healthy and bold.

Five light fabrics were collaged to create a backdrop for the composition. A light stripe was used twice, with the grainlines reversed. Notice that the floral on the right bottom is a larger scale than the other patterns. The vase sits on a yellow plaid lace-trimmed doily which has been set at an angle. Nancy found it necessary to outline the lace with a black button-hole stitch to get it to show against the light background.

The green-and-black bottom inner border is randomly pieced to create a checkerboard. Three of the outside borders are freehand pieced. Follow the yellows around the quilt. Originally the red bottom border was just a wide strip. Even though the fabric was patterned, it felt too plain with the other three pieced borders. The solution was to move Nancy's initials and the year from the bottom of the light background down into the red.

The binding is made from a mixture of fabrics. Notice how Nancy added the yellow area in the bottom right corner to complete the feeling of yellow encircling the quilt.

GROUP QUILTS

Quilts made in a group setting offer a wonderful opportunity to create a folk art quilt. It will definitely be a scrap quilt if you work with contributions from everyone's stash. Even people with little or no quilting experience can contribute to the fun. Components of the composition can be created individually or in teams.

I would suggest the activity for guilds (to make a banner), for wedding and baby showers (more fun than the standard games), and even for special events, like a birthday party or wedding reception. Quilt retreats would also offer an ideal venue, especially when a group is just getting together to work on their own projects. What a fabulous "icebreaker" activity.

Some Suggestions

1. Work with a time limit. This creates a spontaneity that will force people to get beyond their usual reticence.

2. Sew a multi-section pieced background, if possible, before adding the other shapes. This makes it easier to sew the finished piece later. If there are only two background pieces, e.g. foreground and sky, you may want to wait to join the two because you will then have the advantage of temporarily working on a smaller piece. Shapes that straddle the seam will have to be added later.

3. Dictate or brainstorm to determine what shapes should be included. Some preplanning on your part guarantees good results.

4. Items should be pinned, or better yet, basted, in place. A fabric glue stick will also work. Shapes can then be easily sewn later without losing placement.

5. Take a Polaroid® picture so you will have a record for positioning elements, if necessary.

6. Whenever possible, have the artists sew on their own shape. This will save you, or whoever is finishing the quilt, lots of work. Time available and the talent level of participants have to be considered.

7. Plan to have fabric and a permanent marking pen available for a label so you can gather the signatures of all contributors. Use either sandpaper or freezer paper to stabilize the fabric so the writing is more easily accomplished.

8. As with most group projects, learn to accept, in advance, that the workmanship won't be as perfect as if you had done it all yourself. The best part is that the quilt got done!

Label on back of quilt for the Gold Bug Quilters Banner.

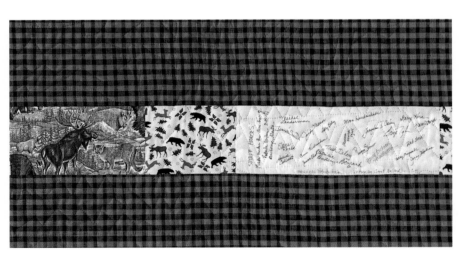

Label sewn in as part of quilt backing for *Eklutna*.

 Fasco Posies

Fasco Posies was created by seventy people on a bus tour who visited Fasco/Fabric Sales in Seattle, following Quilt Market 1996 in Portland, Oregon. Participants were from eight countries and the United States. Seven "quilt husbands" were included. My job was to entertain this crew for a short period of time, about forty-five minutes to an hour. I was to do a schpeil about using plaids and stripes in quilts. Desperate to think of something new to do, I finally decided that we would make a quilt together. In this way, they would be handling and manipulating the fabric, which was my goal.

Participants were squeezed around eight tables, with one rotary cutter, mat, and stack of fabric per table. (Remember, these people came unprepared to create a quilt.) A

Fasco Posies
53" x 58". 1996. Made under the direction of Roberta Horton. Sewn by Nancy Mahoney. Quilted by Geness Reichert. Collection of Fasco/Fabric Sales of Seattle, Washington.

temporary design wall had been stationed in the front of the room. I created a collage of light plaids for the background. I then cut a vase with a rotary cutter. This was done live, for shock value (people always assume you can't cut into fabric without an official pattern). Table assignments were issued: letters, flowers, stems, and leaves. (I did demonstrate letter cutting to the necessary tables.)

Groups quickly worked as teams to supply me with the necessary parts, which I assembled in the front on the design wall. For fun, some shapes were rejected, and sent back for reworking. The energy level was high as competition developed between the tables. A shared bonding-type experience was had by all. This was great fun, so much so, in fact, that I have since worked the exercise into my Folk Art class, when time allows.

Banner

Let's look at another group-made quilt. I was teaching a 2-day workshop for the Gold Bug Quilters of the Gold Country foothills around Placerville, California. Their effort became a banner for the guild. Ample fabric was available. Since sewing machines were also present, one team got the job of sewing the background together. The exercise was used as a warm-up to the real project that they would create later in the class. Time frame: one morning.

I had brought some light-colored fabrics for the background as my contribution. My hostess had a stack of fabric sample squares she was willing to donate to the effort. They proved perfect for the lettering. Others freely gave their fabric as they followed our lead. Most quilters are generous with their fabric.

Individual participants commented to me that they ended up doing things they didn't think they could do. Sometimes there's an advantage to being in a crowd. You get carried away by the momentum. Actually seeing the quilt quickly created

before your eyes, directly in the fabric, is exhilarating. It was a stress-free way to work into the real assignment for the workshop.

The quilt top was later passed around the guild for both hand and raw edge appliqué. Quilting was also a shared task, some doing it by hand and others by machine.

Banner
53" x 43". 1997. Gold Bug Quilters under the direction of Roberta Horton, Placerville, California.

Eats at Olds
50" x 42". 1997.
Made under the
direction of
Roberta Horton
at Olds Fibre
Week, Olds,
Alberta, Canada.
Quilted by Janet
Dollard.

 Eats at Olds

Eats at Olds was created at Fibre Week 1997 held at Olds College, Alberta, Canada. Many of the students lived in residence, so we had a common shared experience—the dining hall. I decided this would make a fun topic for which we could use simple, familiar shapes. Remember, I had to make this decision before I went to the event so I could take some appropriate fabric. I had no idea what the campus looked like, so I decided I needed to pick a not-too-specific topic.

I packed wallpaper and table top fabrics. (The walls turned out to be painted and the tables were formica.) I put in a blue checkerboard fabric for a place mat. (We ate on trays!) Deviations from reality are called "artistic license." I began the quilt by putting up the wallpaper and table top. I then cut the tray. Suddenly, everyone knew the subject of the quilt because of the unique shape of the tray.

As a group we decided what other shapes were needed. Laughs were shared as we recounted the rules. Three beverages were allowed per meal (the green kiwi juice was a wonderful color). French fries were

frequently present, as were carrots. One tiny dessert could be chosen. You can see that the person in our scenario selected three items, so she got "the lecture."

Each class member was given an assignment. Later, they were also asked to stitch their design during class. This enabled participants to try some of the techniques I had been discussing. We could also practice bordering, with each student contributing a fabric. Our quilt is five sided because my hastily picked table fragment proved to have a cut out of it. We agreed that, yes, we had all made four-sided quilts before and we were ready for a new adventure.

Eklutna. Photos by Roberta Horton.

The aforementioned quilts are all relatively simple. More complex quilts will require more preplanning on your part. It's still important that people do their own work and be involved in the decision-making process. As a facilitator, you **should not** provide patterns. Using a pattern makes the effort more like work. It also takes away the joy of discovering that as a group they can create something original.

 Eklutna

I have taught in Anchorage, Alaska, four or five times. On one of my visits I was taken to see the cemetery at Eklutna (Ee-kloot-na). It is a Tanaina (or Dena'ina) Athabascan Indian village one-half hour north of Anchorage. (The location is now a historical park.)

The brightly colored "spirit houses" are an Athabascan burial tradition meshed with Russian Orthodox beliefs. Before the Russian missionaries arrived, the Indians cremated their dead, which released a person's breath spirit to the sky and their shadow spirit to the underground. With the adoption of a new religion, the bodies were buried (which interfered with the release of the spirits). The spirit house on top of a grave now provides a place for the spirits to reside. Some families use a specific color to identify their clan. A three-barred Orthodox cross in front of a Spirit House denotes church membership.

I was very touched by this cemetery and wanted to do a quilt capturing what I had seen. My own grandfather was from Russia. I always seem to get in touch with that part of myself when I visit Alaska, which has such a strong Russian heritage. I got bogged down in how I would execute the quilt. Frankly, I just got too complicated in my thoughts, so I filed everything in the "back burner" area of my mind. When I learned I was to return again to Anchorage to do a Folk Art Workshop for the Log Cabin Quilters, my ideas resurfaced. Folk art would be a perfect format, and I had found that the guild would take on anything. Did I have the nerve to ask them?

After showing slides of folk art, I stuck in some of Eklutna. I had brought some great sky fabric with

me and confiscated some green fabric from a class member (a guild tradition). These went up on the design wall. I then proceeded to build the blue spirit house. In advance, I had selected the easiest one to do from memory. We looked at the slides again, this time analyzing how simple the shapes were. Participants broke up into committees:

- two spirit houses
- one prayer chapel
  (replica of one in Siberia)
- flowers
- trees
- letters

Eklutna
53" x 58". 1997. Made under the direction of Roberta Horton by the Log Cabin Quilters, Anchorage, Alaska. Quilted by Janet Dollard.

At some point, a talented class member walked up with the mountains cut from a wonderful fabric. I later satin stitched the composition. I added three trees in the center area of the quilt, making sure to work in the same style and being sure to repeat two already-used fabrics. I was thinking ahead to the quilting, and trying to figure out how I might fill in such a large blank area with stitches. *Eklutna* doesn't have as many buildings as the real location. Yet I think it does capture the feeling of what I saw. I love the result!

International Quilt Festival

The International Quilt Festival in Houston, Texas, provided an opportunity to create another group quilt. Many quilters from around the world look forward to attending this annual event in the fall each year. After selecting the topic from several choices, we as a class decided on the following categories:

- letters
- QUILTS
- prize ribbons
- quilters
- tote bags or baskets of goodies
- FOOD COURT

The quilt itself was composed in only one hour and ten minutes. Lettering had been demonstrated and practiced first to give necessary skills and confidence to the participants. Then it was announced that they would be making a quilt together. Don't scare off the participants by letting them know too soon what you expect of them. A non-threatening warm-up activity or exercise is essential to build confidence when you don't know the ability level of your audience. A kind class member volunteered to sew and quilt our masterpiece.

International Quilt Festival
37" x 57". 1997. Made under the direction of Roberta Horton in Houston, Texas. Sewn and quilted by Tonee White.

SKiLLS

6

For a few minutes,

suspend your self doubts

and do as I say—

FORGet

the word **can't**

—and try these few

exercises.

You must really do them.

Reading them is

not good enough.

Before we begin, I want you to consider my statement: "When a block of marble is delivered to the sculptor, the statue is already in that piece of stone. The sculptor has only to chip away the unnecessary parts to reveal the form." Once you accept this fact, you're on your way to creating your own patterns.

Another way to state the above: Determine the size rectangle which is necessary to contain the desired shape.

CReating YOUR OWN APPLIQUÉ Patterns

EXERcise I.
Letters

The easiest way to test my principle is to try to create your name in block letters. On plain paper draw two parallel horizontal lines 3" apart. Connect the lines with vertical lines 2" apart. Spacing between the letters will be added when the shapes are positioned on the quilt. (Your blocks of marble are 2" wide and 3" high.)

Step 1. Draw Letters

1. With a pencil, using the outside edge of the rectangle as a guide, "chip off" the unnecessary pieces to spell your name in upper-case letters. Make sure your letter shapes are fat enough. Look at my example.

2. Now create your name in lower-case letters. You can use the same size rectangles or you can make them shorter. Some lower-case letter shapes are more appealing than the upper-case versions.

3. Cut out the paper letters, picking the version of each letter you like best. Arrange the letters on the table, adding the proper spacing between them. For a folk art feeling, upper- and lower-case letters can be combined in the same word. Whether you realize it or not, your lettering style matches itself. My shapes will differ from yours. This is both okay and desirable, as you have your own personal style and I have mine.

Supplies:

1. plain white paper (lined or graph paper will keep your right brain from being creative)

2. pencil with eraser (ink pens are permanent and don't allow you to change your mind)

3. paper scissors that fit your hands well (they don't have to be able to cut fabric)

4. good quality fabric scissors with sharp points (my favorite are 7" Gingher™ shears)

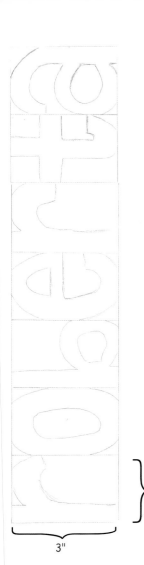

Step 2. Cut Letters Directly in Paper

The next step is to try cutting the letters from paper without drawing them first. Cut a stack of 2" x 3" paper rectangles. Proceed in the exact same manner, this time using your paper scissors, rather than a pencil, to do the chipping.

When you want to hand appliqué, it will be necessary to add a seam allowance that can be turned under as you sew. Pin your paper pattern to the fabric; add the seam allowance by eye as you cut out the shape. Remember, any irregularities in cutting give character to the shape.

Step 3. Cut Letters Directly in Fabric

Once you see how well this works, your rectangles can become actual pieces of fabric. Remember: Cutting directly in the fabric gives you shapes without a seam allowance. Therefore, you will need to use a satin stitch or raw-edge appliqué technique (see Appliqué Sewing Methods, page 125) when attaching your motif to the background of your quilt.

When you want to hand appliqué, it will be necessary to add a seam allowance that can be turned under as you sew.

Tribute
36" x 19". 1997. Jacqueline Carley, Anchorage, Alaska. Can you decipher Jackie's message?

EXERCISE II.
SIMPLE SHAPES

The next step is applying this expertise to other shapes.

Step 1. Symmetrical Shape

For practice, let's work with a simple heart shape. Fold your paper in half. Always start and end your cutting at the fold. Remember to use the edge of the paper as a guide to obtain the correct size.

Step 2. Asymmetrical Shape

Next, let's try an asymmetrical heart. This time don't fold the paper in half. Mentally determine the middle line and start cutting here as you previously did. Cut the first half of the heart, then continue on to the second half. You will notice that the first half doesn't exactly match the second half. Good!

Step 3. Critique

Compare your two hearts. The asymmetrical heart is more irregular than the symmetrical heart. It therefore has a more unique personality than the predictable symmetrical heart. This rendering is more appropriate if you are aiming for a folk art feeling for your quilt.

Step 4. Multiple Units

Now, cut several more hearts from the same size paper. Compare these. Each one is different and will guarantee more energy for your quilt. Therefore, I suggest that when a repetitive shape is used, each one should be individually cut rather than using a template repetitively. You should also see that the next logical step is to cut this simple heart shape right in the fabric.

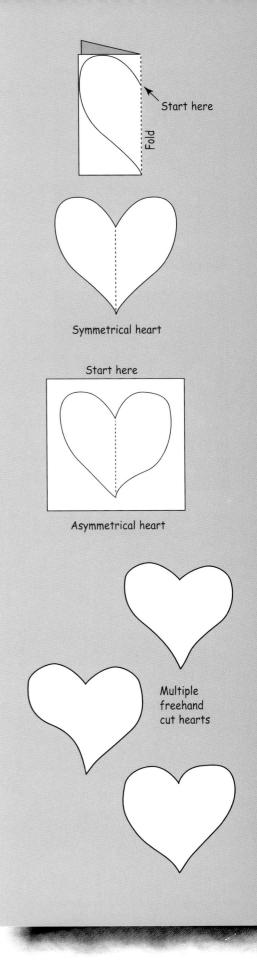

Start here

Fold

Symmetrical heart

Start here

Asymmetrical heart

Multiple freehand cut hearts

Symmetrical and asymmetrical women

MORE COMPLICATED FAMILIAR SHAPES

I suggest paper cutting a pattern when you want to create more complex shapes. Once you have your basic outline, cut the shape apart to create templates for the various areas to be done in different fabrics.

Step 1. Symmetrical Person

Fold your paper in half and cut a female human figure. Follow these instructions: Start with the head, which brings you back to the center for the neck, then out for the shoulders which extend into the arms (forget about a hand for now). Continue back to the torso which will nip in at the waist, then flare out for a skirt. As you complete the bottom of the skirt, legs with shoes will be cut which will get you back to the skirt bottom, and the center fold. Open out your creation.

Step 2. Asymmetrical Person

Don't fold the paper. This time cut down one side and then up the other side of your figure. On purpose, try to add some animation. The hairdo can be at different angles on the two sides. The arms can be in different positions; the same for the legs. The skirt can even show movement. Compare your two women.

EXERCISE IV.
DESIGN SOURCE FOR PAPER CUTTING

Sometimes you will find it helpful to have a reference picture, or design source, to look at as you cut a desired shape. Drawings are easier to use than photographs, which show dimension.

1. Just as before, start with a piece of paper the desired finished size.

2. With the design source on a table in front of you, line up your eyes and your scissors with the design source. You will only be looking straight ahead, watching the perimeter of the design source. Start at the easiest point of entry. Make the first incision.

3. Continually turn the design source as you cut (clockwise for right-handed, counter-clockwise for left-handed), keeping your eyes and scissors in line with the outside edge of the design. Basically, you will only be making straight, or at the most, slightly curved cuts. The drawings here are an example of the turns you would make to create this bird shape. Cutting right-handed, you will notice that the bird starts out horizontal because that seems to be the easiest place to enter the shape. The bird's legs could be done as a second stage.

4. Now you have the basic outline of your pattern. Next, you will need to find fabric that fits your needs, realizing that the appliqué shape may change to fit the fabric.

5. Experiment with placement.

Separately cut birds all one direction.

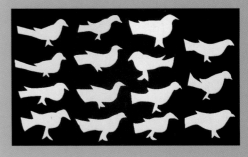

One bird's direction reversed is noticeable.

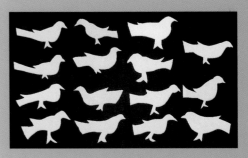

Several turned birds aren't as noticeable and give energy to the composition.

Design source: bird

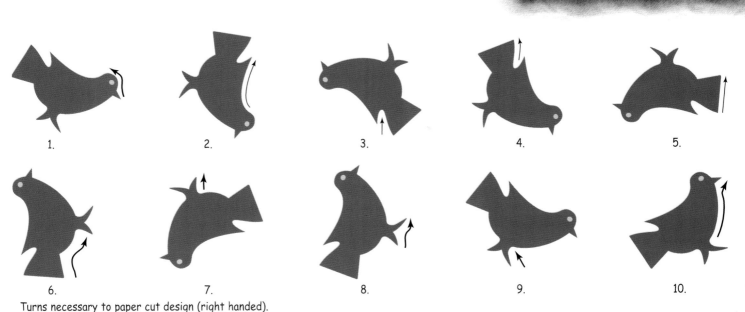

Turns necessary to paper cut design (right handed).

SUMMARY

Here is the general procedure for creating appliqué shapes:

1. Cut a rectangle of plain white paper to what you think is the desired size.

2. Place the rectangle on the quilt background, which is pinned on the design wall. Step back and look at the piece of paper in relation to the other shapes. Does the size feel right, or is it too big or too small? Make the necessary adjustments to the rectangle.

3. Now whittle away to reveal the shape. Use any of the before-mentioned techniques to create the shape. Remember to cut toward the outside edges of the paper to keep the shape the right size. The tendency is to cut small shapes in the center of the paper. Big is better.

4. Place the paper-cut shape on the quilt. Make any necessary adjustments.

5. Cut the shape in fabric. This will immediately transport you from an old-fashioned black and white movie to wonderful Technicolor.

Note: A rectangle of fabric may be substituted for the paper rectangle in Steps 1-4. Remember, these fabric shapes will not have seam allowances.

Appliqué Sewing Methods

Now that you know how to create your own original appliqué shapes, it's time to think about how you want to sew them. Fortunately, there are many ways to appliqué. Each method has distinct advantages and disadvantages.

Machine Satin Stitch

(no seam allowance required)

1. Adjust the width and length of the stitch for the specific project, depending on the desired effect. Stitches should be wide and close enough together to prevent fraying.

2. The top thread tension should be loosened. Some machines, like a Bernina™, need to have the bobbin thread put through the hole in the arm of the bobbin case.

3. Use 60/2 embroidery thread for the smoothest look.

4. Use a matching thread to make the stitches blend with the fabric or a contrasting thread color to make the stitches accent the fabric.

5. For speed, use one color throughout the project. For visual interest, change the thread color, which takes time but is visually more exciting.

Advantage: Holds up better than raw-edge appliqué.

Disadvantages: Have to use a zigzag machine.

Uses a lot of thread.

Raw-Edge Appliqué

(no seam allowance required)

1. Sew a line of very small, straight machine stitches around the perimeter of the shape 1/16" to 1/4" in from the edge using regular sewing thread (50/3).

2. Stitch around each shape **twice**. On the second trip around, stitch with a regular length stitch, a zigzag stitch, or free-form machine doodle. Or, the second row can be added when you machine quilt. You can use a different thread color or a different type of thread, like Sulky® rayon, for the second stitching.

Advantage: Requires the least sewing machine expertise.

Frayed edge will add texture, giving a more primitive look.

Disadvantage: Edges will fray.

Least sturdy method.

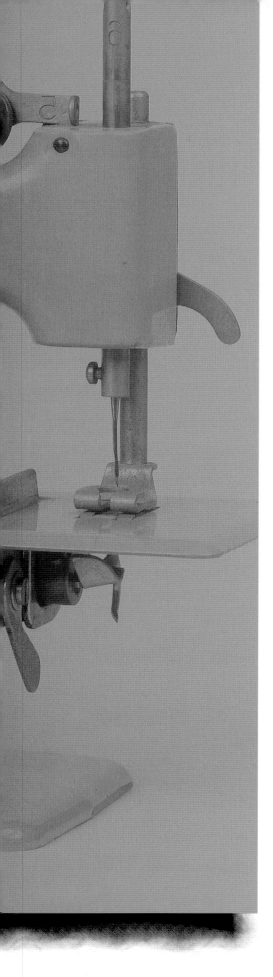

Machine Appliqué Recommendations
(satin stitch and straight stitch raw-edge)

1. Beginners should stiffen appliqué shapes with one of the following:

   a. A wash-away fabric stabilizer such as Perfect Sew™. Follow the directions on the bottle. Work on aluminum foil or waxed paper to avoid messing up your work surface. Wash in lukewarm water to remove stiffness (fabric needs to be prewashed).

   b. Spray starch; then iron.

2. To adhere appliqué shapes to background:

   a. Hand baste.

   b. Dab on wash-away fabric stabilizer; heat-set in place with iron.

   c. Use a fabric glue stick sparingly to attach appliqué shape to background. Glue is temporary, so may have to be reapplied. It works best on small areas.

3. The background fabric must be stabilized to prevent puckering and tunneling as you stitch. This is always true for satin stitch. I use a tear-away stabilizer on the underneath side of the background fabric. It's literally torn away when you have completed the stitching. There are several brands and weights (lighter is better), so experiment until you find the one you like. The product may vary with the selected stitch and the weight of the background fabric. I like:

     Mark Textiles Appliqué Tear-Away®
     Sulky Easy-Tear™
     Sulky Totally Stable™ (Iron-on Tear Away Stabilizer)
     Thread Pro™ Stitch & Ditch™ Stabilizer (paper)

4. Use an open-toe presser foot if you're doing a satin, zigzag, or decorative stitch. This allows you to see what you're doing.

5. Using the right needle type and size can make a big difference. You will have to do some experimenting with your machine, the various types and brands of thread, and the fabric that you're using. Someone else can be using the exact same model sewing machine you are, with identical fabric and thread as yours and have different results. It must have something to do with how fast you sew and how you position and move your hands. For most projects, I use a Schmetz Jeans/Denim 80/12.

Hand Appliqué

(seam allowance required)

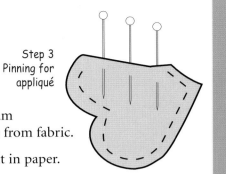

Step 3
Pinning for
appliqué

1. Shape cutting options:

    a. Cut the shape first in paper. Add the seam allowance later when you cut the shape from fabric.

Disadvantage: You temporarily see the quilt in paper.

    b. Cut the shape in fabric without seam allowance so you can compose the quilt. Re-cut the shape a second time, adding the seam allowance, when you're ready to sew.

    Advantage: Allows you to see the shape in fabric, in the correct size, as you compose the quilt.

Disadvantage: If you're working with a unique fabric, or a limited amount, there might not be enough extra to have the luxury of cutting it twice.

2. Using an X or a straight line, baste the shape to the background. Don't bother to baste all the way around the edge.

3. Turn under the seam allowance (I prefer a skinny ¼") and hold it in place with pins placed perpendicular to the edge. Only work on a 2" or 3" section at a time. Do your pinning on a flat surface. Check the back periodically to see that you aren't creating a bubble under the shape.

4. Use a hidden hemming stitch, with thread matching the appliqué fabric. Stitches should be about ⅛" apart. Be sure to pull the thread snugly.

5. Convex curved areas (those that protrude) will need some fullness eased in because you're turning a larger area into a smaller area. Turn under the seam allowance and feel for lumps. Place the piece flat on your work table. Position your fingers on both sides of the lumpy area. Run the sharp end of a needle under the seam allowance, pulling gently up toward you. The tension created will allow you to redistribute the fullness. Pin. (Never clip this type of curve!)

6. Concave curves (those that dip into the shape) may require clipping to release the tension as you turn under the seam allowance from a smaller area into a larger area. Cuts should be less than the ¼" seam allowance. Make a minimum of cuts; it's better to have to add more if the curve is still too tight. Make stitches closer together in this area.

7. Turning corners is done in three stages. Fold under the seam allowance to the end of one side and trim any fabric that extends beyond the other side. Next, fold under a triangle at the tip; stitch to the point. Finally, fold under the second side's seam allowance. Put more stitches at the corners to firmly anchor them.

    Advantage: Very sturdy.

                      Gives a traditional finished look to the project.

Disadvantage: Most time-consuming method.

                      Requires more hand dexterity.

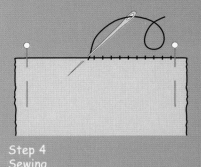

Step 4
Sewing

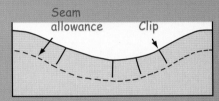

Step 5
Convex Curves

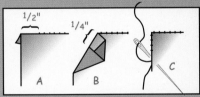

Step 6
Concave Curves

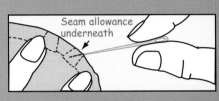

Step 7
Right Angle Corners;

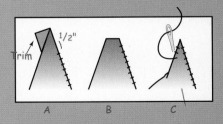

Step 7
Turning Corners With Sharp Points

DRAFTING PIECED PATTERNS

You need to know only two things to be able to draft pieced patterns. The first is to be able to recognize what grid format is used for the pattern; the second is to know how to change the finished size of the block.

DRAFTING THE PATTERN

Drafting decisions aren't made arbitrarily; usually some logical and easily-seen reference point acts as a guide. Most pieced patterns are based on a square divided into a given number of equal-size units. To establish the grid size, look for the tiniest unit and then see how many times you can divide it into one side. The illustration below shows the most common grids with a pattern below each one made from that grid.

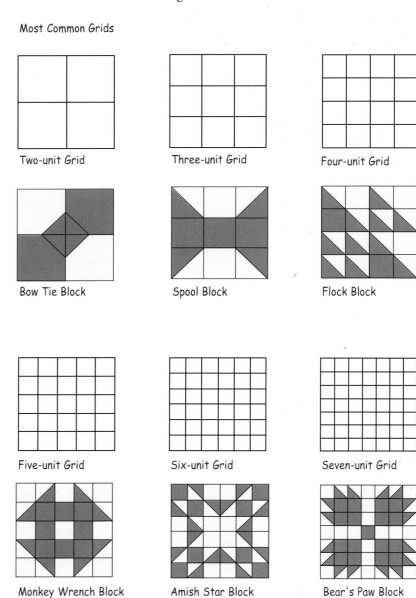

Most Common Grids

Two-unit Grid Three-unit Grid Four-unit Grid

Bow Tie Block Spool Block Flock Block

Five-unit Grid Six-unit Grid Seven-unit Grid

Monkey Wrench Block Amish Star Block Bear's Paw Block

When making templates from the drafted pattern, it isn't essential to use all the lines of the original grid. Try to make each shape as large as possible, in essence erasing unnecessary lines. Don't create more work for yourself than is necessary. Add ¼" seam allowance to all sides of each shape. I mark on each template both the number of pieces that need to be cut for one block and the correct value information (L indicating that piece needs to be cut from light fabric, M for medium, D for dark). Remember, in a scrap quilt the information doesn't always stay the same.

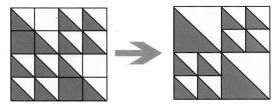

Make each shape as large as possible.

CHANGING THE SIZE OF THE BLOCK

Use the following method to make any size block:

1. Use a ruler and a right-angle to draw a square the desired finished size on plain paper. Label the corners A B C D.

2. Using a ruler as a reference, identify the next number past the length of one side of your square that the grid number will divide into evenly. Let's call that number M (for magic).

3. Position the left-hand end of the ruler (zero) in the bottom left-hand corner (A). Using A as a pivot point, move the ruler up the opposite side (B/C) of the square until it intersects M, your magic number.

4. Divide M by the grid number. Using the resulting number, mark dots along the ruler at these evenly-divided intervals.

5. Position a right-angle so one side is on the bottom line (A/B) and the adjacent side touches a dot. Now draw a perpendicular line that connects A/B to C/D. Do this for each interval dot. The square is now divided into equal intervals going in one direction.

6. Turn the paper one-quarter turn, making B/C the bottom line. Repeat steps 3 through 5 to get your second set of lines. You now have the necessary grid upon which to fill in your pattern.

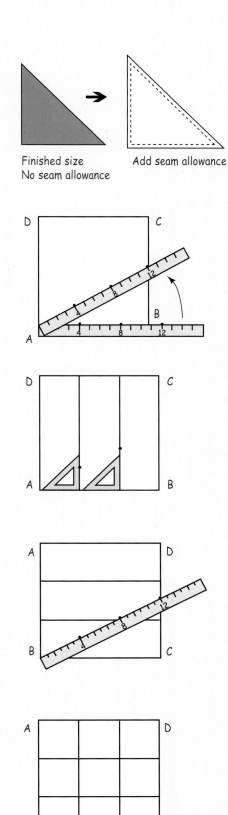

Finished size
No seam allowance

Add seam allowance

Division of space into given number of equal units.

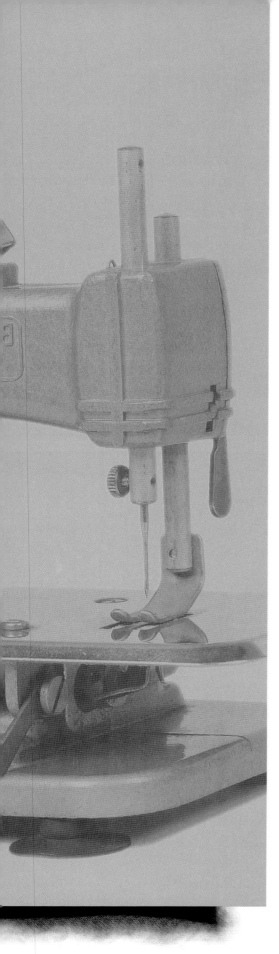

Creative Piecing

It's possible to be as free with piecing as it is with appliqué. For *Frau Horton, Frau Horton* on page 98 I wanted to create some pieced figures. I made a simple pencil sketch of what the dolls/women might look like. You will notice I didn't draw on graph paper. I wanted each woman to be original, so I didn't want an exact pattern. I wanted my figures to be spontaneous and filled with energy.

The sketch defined the basic shapes for me. Each unit was comprised of four strips:

- head, hair/hat, and background

- arms, bodice, and background

- skirt with apron and background

- legs with shoes and background

Seam allowance had to be added when I cut out each piece. Each finished unit was a surprise and spurred me on to make the next lady. Some of the seams were curved. No templates were used.

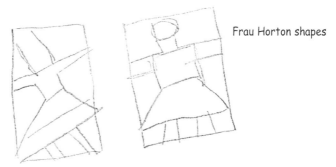

Frau Horton shapes

Free-Form Piecing

1. Make a rough sketch of the desired shape on plain white paper.

2. Determine how the picture can be divided into sewable rows. Simplify if necessary.

3. Cut individual shapes in fabric, adding seam allowance as you cut.

4. The finished shapes will vary in size. Trim to fit in the desired area.

Option: Motif can be inserted with a curved seam into the composition.

Quilt label on *Sundogs Over Susitna..* For full quilt see page 100.

CURVED SEAM PIECING

1. Position two fabrics right side up on top of each other. *(Note: No seam allowance has been added for the cut edges. Cut these fabric pieces larger than needed, then trim to the desired size after sewing.)*

2. Use a rotary cutter to cut a curving line through the two fabrics.

3. Carefully remove the top right-hand piece and the lower left-hand piece. The curved edge will match on the two remaining fabric pieces.

4. Carefully turn fabrics to the wrong side, keeping the curve in alignment. Mark several short pencil lines across the cut onto both fabrics. These will serve as sewing notches.

5. Position the fabrics right sides together along the curve. Match and pin at the top and bottom, as well as at the notches. Sew with ¼" seam allowance.

Cut a curving line.

Remove top right-hand and lower left-hand pieces.

Notch

Notch

Notch

Turn to wrong side and mark notches.

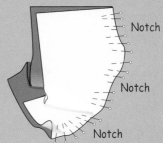

Notch

Notch

Notch

Position right sides together and pin.

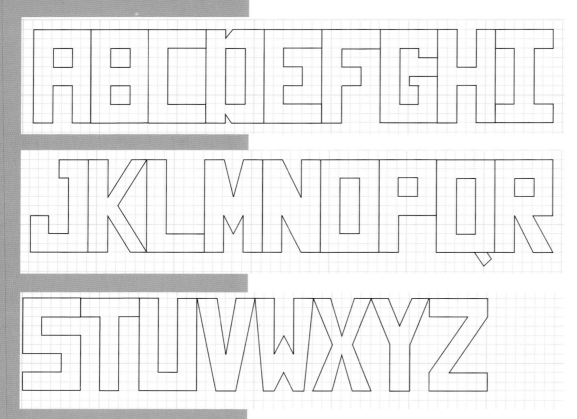

Draw the letters using the grid.

PieCeD BLoCK LeTTeRS

1. Determine the size of the letters. Draw the units on graph paper.

2. Draw the letters using the grid as a reference.

3. Determine the common background fabric. Select one fabric for all parts of each letter. This will ensure legibility.

4. Use a quilter's ruler to cut the required fabric shapes; add the necessary seam allowances to each piece.

5. Use background fabric to add spaces between letters. Larger spaces will be required between words. Sew.

Hints for Machine Piecing

1. Be sure to use the appropriate needle. I use Schmetz Jeans/Denim 80/12.

2. If you use a zigzag machine, make these changes:

   a. Use special ¼" foot, not the standard foot for zigzag. This will give you greater control.

   b. Use a straight stitch throat plate rather than a zigzag one, so the machine won't chew up the beginning of the seam. You will also experience greater control.

Throat plates for zigzag and straight stitching.

Quilting

The act of adding the quilting stitches to your composition brings it alive. Pay attention to what you're doing. Truthfully, you're at the most only halfway done when you finish your quilt top!

Traditional quilts frequently employ the use of a grid for the quilting design. Study the chart below. Notice how the designs get more complex. The spacing between the lines will be determined by your quilt. I usually start with a 1" grid. You may find that a ½" grid works better for a particular project.

It will also make a difference whether the lines of your grid are parallel or diagonal to the edge of the quilt. Parallel is static, whereas diagonal gives a feeling of movement. Try it both ways.

I suggest making a permanent set of grids for auditioning. Use acetate (from an art supply store) and a permanent marking pen to create the different patterns, one sheet of acetate per design. These grids can be laid on top of the quilt top. Work from simple to complex. I suggest laying the first two side by side. Remove the one you like the least, replacing it with the next in order. Move through the set until all have been tried. The answer may surprise you.

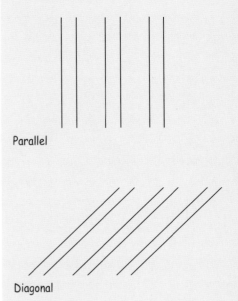

Parallel

Diagonal

Diamonds are another possibility. Here is a simple way to create diamonds.

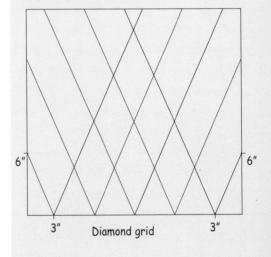

Diamond grid

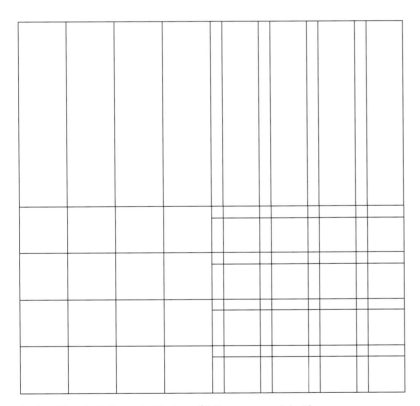

Basic grids: single lines, double lines (¹/4"), square, and double square.

Detail of *San Miguel de Allende*. For full quilt see page 107.

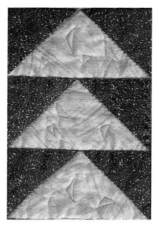

Detail of *Corroboree*. Machine quilted triangles

Detail of *Corroboree*. Hand quilting technique.

Whenever possible, I use the fabric or the subject matter of the quilt as an inspiration. Helen Cummins used some of the grids to fill in areas on the buildings in her scene. She also made up a cobblestone pattern to use under the birds' feet.

I used both machine and hand quilting in *Corroboree* (page 67). Basic machine quilting was done in all the seams. I also added a decorative triangle shape in some of my flying geese triangles. This went through all the layers, so it counts as quilting. It would be the equivalent of tieing, or tacking, a quilt.

Machine quilting felt too strong to go over the surface of the little girls featured in the plain blocks. I opted to hand quilt these units using an irregular curved line. A bone bead was added periodically. They were sewn on with the quilting thread as I was executing the quilting stitches. I felt the need for a simple embellishment.

A FEW FINAL WORDS

Keep your creative options open as you go through the various stages of making your quilt. Do a lot of auditioning and experimenting as you build your quilt. Pay attention to all the choices, including the backing, binding, and even the quilt label. Don't always be satisfied with the most obvious solution. Learn to follow your instincts by honoring that little voice inside you that nudges you toward the right choice—or a different choice. One of the best things you can say about a finished quilt is, "How unlike me that I made that quilt."

Detail of *Corroboree* Quilt label.

BLOCK PATTERNS

The following blocks can be drafted any size using the instructions on page 129, or enlarged on a photocopy machine as follows. Be sure you use a photocopy machine that does not distort the block.

6" Block: Enlarge 200%.

9" Block: Enlarge 200%, then 150%.

12" Block: Enlarge 200%, then 200%.

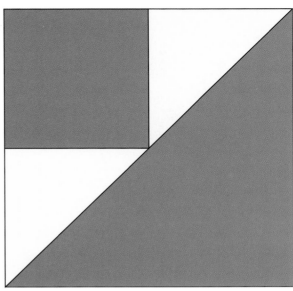

Angles and Squares

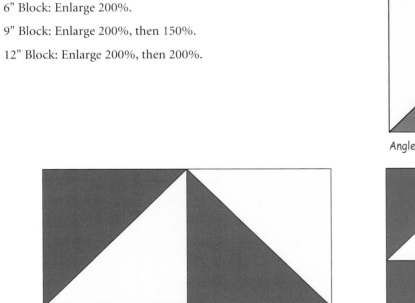

Broken Dishes

Birds in Flight

Shoo-fly

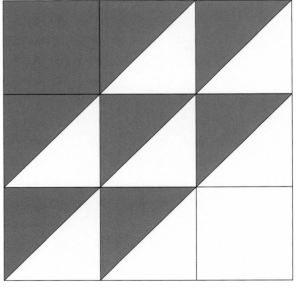

Northwind

Bound for Kobe

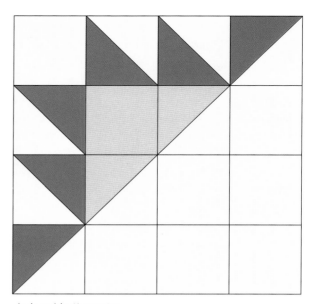

Delectable Mountains

Gem Block

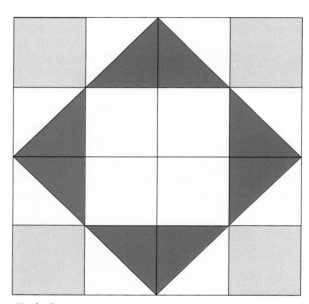

King's Crown

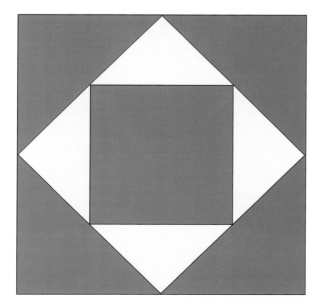

Squares in Squares

Square on Square

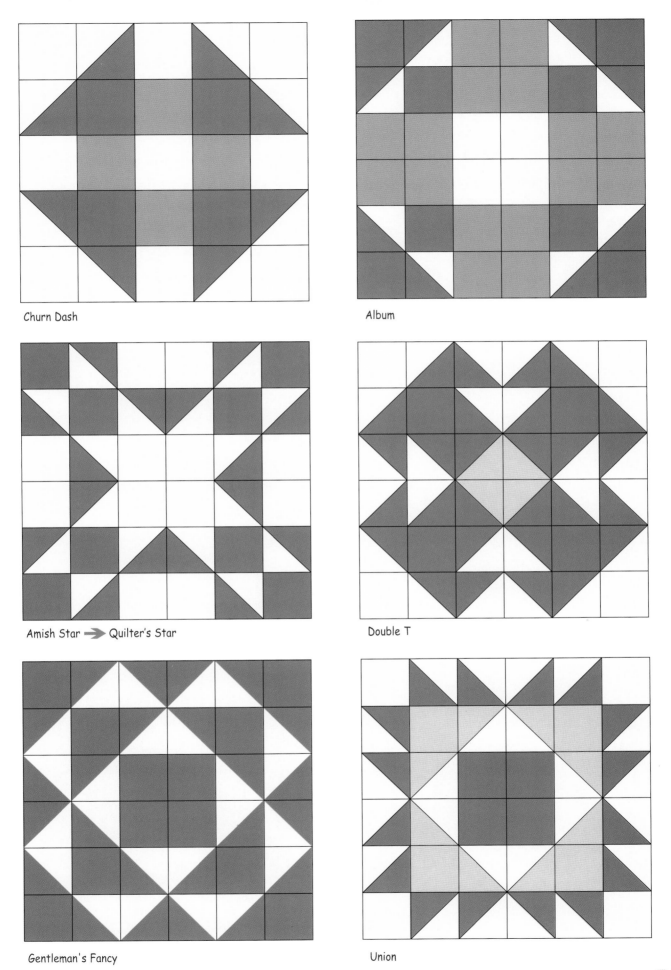

Churn Dash

Album

Amish Star ➡ Quilter's Star

Double T

Gentleman's Fancy

Union

137

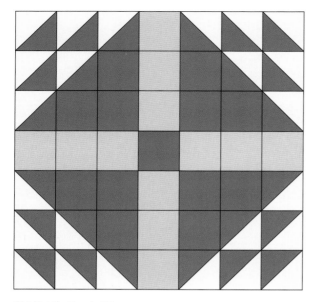

Old Maid's Puzzle II

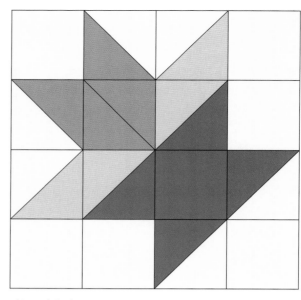

(Scrap) Basket

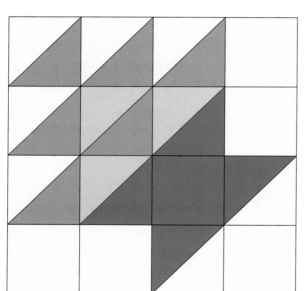

Simple Flower Basket

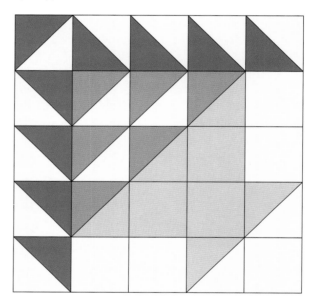

Dolly's Basket

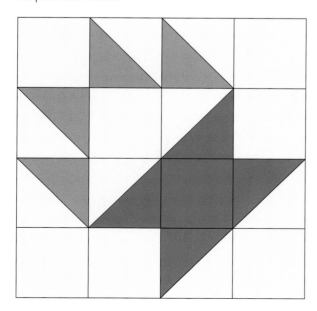

Cake Stand

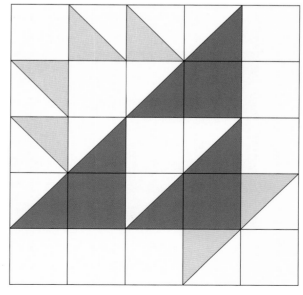

Flower Pot

BiBLioGRaPHY

Pieced Patterns Using Rotary Cutting

Hopkins, Judy.
Around the Block with Judy Hopkins.
Bothell, WA: That Patchwork Place,
1994.

Johnson-Srebro, Nancy.
Measure the Possibilities with Omnigrid. Burlington, WA: Omnigrid®
Inc., 1993.

Martin, Judy.
The Block Book. Grinnell, IA:
Crosley-Griffith Publishing, Inc.,
1998.

Martin, Judy.
*Judy Martin's Ultimate Rotary Cutting
Reference.* Grinnell, IA: Crosley-Griffith Publishing, Inc., 1997.

Techniques

Bolton, Janet.
*Patchwork Folk Art: Using Appliqué
& Quilting Techniques.* New York:
Sterling Publishing Co., Inc., 1995.

Hargrave, Harriet.
*Heirloom Machine Quilting: A Comprehensive Guide to Hand-Quilted
Effects Using Your Sewing Machine.*
Lafayette, CA: C&T Publishing, 1995.

Hargrave, Harriet.
Mastering Machine Appliqué.
Lafayette, CA: C&T Publishing, 1991.

Johnson, Vicki.
Paint and Patches. Paducah, KY:
American Quilters Society, 1995.

Noble, Maurine.
Machine Quilting Made Easy. Bothell,
WA: That Patchwork Place, 1994.

BUYiNG GUiDE

The Cotton Patch Mail Order
3405 Hall Lane, Dept. CTB
Lafayette, CA 94549
e-mail: cottonpa@aol.com
(800) 835-4418
(925) 283-7883
(Reducing glasses, hand-dyed fabrics,
tear-away stabilizers, 60/2 and 50/3
cotton threads)

Hand-dyed Fabrics

Alaska Dyeworks
300 W. Swanson #101
Wasella, AK 99654
Ph/Fax: (907) 373-6562
(800) 478-1755

Sonya Lee Barrington
837 47th Avenue
San Francisco, CA 94121
(415) 221-6510

Shades Hand Dyed Textiles
585 Cobb Parkway, S.
The Nunn Complex, Studio "O"
Marietta, GA 30062-8202
(800) 783-3933
Fax: (770) 919-9854

Skydyes
PO Box 370116
West Hartford, CT 06137-0116
(740) 232-1429
Fax: (740) 236-9117

Lunn Fabrics
317 E. Main St
Lancaster, OH 43130
(614) 654-2202
Fax: (614) 654-3949
http://www.lunnfabrics.com

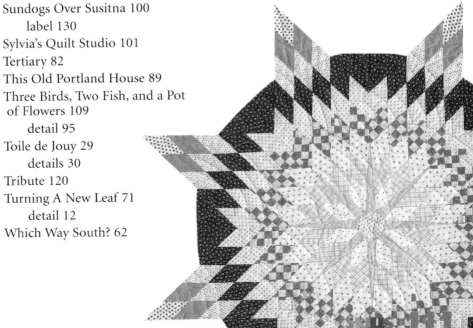

ABOUT THE AUTHOR

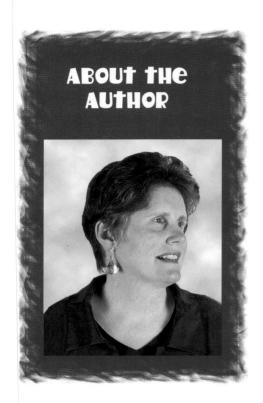

Scrap Quilts: The Art of Making Do is Roberta Horton's sixth book about making quilts. Roberta began her sewing career at the age of ten when she learned to make clothes for her dolls. She continued her study of textiles through her B.S. degree in Home Economics from the University of California at Berkeley. After five years of public high school teaching, Roberta retired and began her second career as a quiltmaker.

Combining her love of fabric with her love of teaching, Roberta taught the first state-accredited class in quiltmaking in California in 1973. Her personal goal was to teach, and eventually to write, disclosing what she had discovered about quiltmaking. This passion has taken Roberta to Canada, Japan, New Zealand, Australia, The Netherlands, Denmark, Germany, Norway, England, France, Belgium, and South Africa as well as across the United States. Whenever possible, Roberta has delved into the history of fabric and tracked down quilts and their makers, broadening her own knowledge and understanding of the wonderful world of quilts.

Roberta's work has appeared in numerous quilt magazines and books. She designs fabric for Fasco/Fabric Sales of Seattle and was selected as one of the 88 most influential quiltmakers in the world by Nihon Vogue, publisher of *Quilts Japan*.

For information on workshops and lectures, write to Roberta Horton, 1929 El Dorado Avenue, Berkeley, California 94707-2404.

OTHER FINE BOOKS FROM C&T PUBLISHING

An Amish Adventure, 2nd Edition, Roberta Horton

Anatomy of a Doll, The Fabric Sculptor's Handbook, Susanna Oroyan

Appliqué 12 Easy Ways! Elly Sienkiewicz

Art & Inspirations, Ruth B. McDowell, Ruth B. McDowell

The Art of Silk Ribbon Embroidery, Judith Baker Montano

The Artful Ribbon, Candace Kling

Baltimore Album Legacy, Catalog of C&T Publishing's 1998 Baltimore Album Quilt Show and Contest, Elly Sienkiewicz

Baltimore Beauties and Beyond (Volume I), Elly Sienkiewicz

Basic Seminole Patchwork, Cheryl Greider Bradkin

Beyond the Horizon, Small Landscape Appliqué, Valerie Hearder

Buttonhole Stitch Appliqué, Jean Wells

A Colorful Book, Yvonne Porcella

Colors Changing Hue, Yvonne Porcella

Crazy Quilt Handbook, Judith Montano

Crazy Quilt Odyssey, Judith Montano

Crazy with Cotton, Diana Leone

Curves in Motion, Quilt Designs & Techniques, Judy B. Dales

Deidre Scherer, Work in Fabric and Thread, Deidre Scherer

Dimensional Appliqué, Baskets, Blooms & Baltimore Borders, Elly Sienkiewicz

Easy Pieces, Creative Color Play with Two Simple Quilt Blocks, Margaret J. Miller

Elegant Stitches, An Illustrated Stitch Guide & Source Book of Inspiration, Judith Baker Montano

Enduring Grace, Quilts from the Shelburne Museum Collection, Celia Y. Oliver

Everything Flowers, Quilts from the Garden, Jean and Valori Wells

The Fabric Makes the Quilt, Roberta Horton

Faces & Places, Images in Appliqué, Charlotte Warr Andersen

Fantastic Figures, Ideas & Techniques Using the New Clays, Susanna Oroyan

Focus on Features, Life-like Portrayals in Appliqué, Charlotte Warr Andersen

Forever Yours, Wedding Quilts, Clothing & Keepsakes, Amy Barickman

Fractured Landscape Quilts, Katie Pasquini Masopust

Free Stuff for Quilters on the Internet, Judy Heim and Gloria Hansen

From Fiber to Fabric, The Essential Guide to Quiltmaking Textiles, Harriet Hargrave

Hand Quilting with Alex Anderson, Six Projects for Hand Quilters

Heirloom Machine Quilting, Third Edition, Harriet Hargrave

Imagery on Fabric, Second Edition, Jean Ray Laury

Impressionist Palette, Gai Perry

Impressionist Quilts, Gai Perry

Jacobean Rhapsodies, Composing with 28 Appliqué Designs, Patricia B. Campbell and Mimi Ayars

Judith B. Montano, Art & Inspirations, Judith B. Montano

Kaleidoscopes & Quilts, Paula Nadelstern

Mariner's Compass Quilts, New Directions, Judy Mathieson

Mastering Machine Appliqué, Harriet Hargrave

Michael James, Art & Inspirations, Michael James

The New Sampler Quilt, Diana Leone

On the Surface, Thread Embellishment & Fabric Manipulation, Wendy Hill

Papercuts and Plenty, Vol. III of Baltimore Beauties and Beyond, Elly Sienkiewicz

Patchwork Persuasion, Fascinating Quilts from Traditional Designs, Joen Wolfrom

Patchwork Quilts Made Easy, Jean Wells (co-published with Rodale Press, Inc.)

Pattern Play, Doreen Speckmann

Pieced Clothing Variations, Yvonne Porcella

Pieces of an American Quilt, Patty McCormick

Piecing, Expanding the Basics, Ruth B. McDowell

Plaids & Stripes, The Use of Directional Fabrics in Quilts, Roberta Horton

Quilts for Fabric Lovers, Alex Anderson

Quilts from the Civil War, Nine Projects, Historical Notes, Diary Entries, Barbara Brackman

Quilts, Quilts, and More Quilts! Diana McClun and Laura Nownes

Recollections, Judith Baker Montano

RIVA, If Ya Wanna Look Good, Honey, Your Feet Gotta Hurt..., Ruth Reynolds

Say It with Quilts, Diana McClun and Laura Nownes

Simply Stars, Quilts that Sparkle, Alex Anderson

Six Color World, Color, Cloth, Quilts & Wearables, Yvonne Porcella

Small Scale Quiltmaking, Precision, Proportion, and Detail, Sally Collins

Soft-Edge Piecing, Jinny Beyer

Start Quilting with Alex Anderson, Six Projects for First-Time Quilters, Alex Anderson

Stripes in Quilts, Mary Mashuta

Tradition with a Twist, Variations on Your Favorite Quilts, Blanche Young and Dalene Young Stone

Trapunto by Machine, Hari Walner

The Visual Dance, Creating Spectacular Quilts, Joen Wolfrom

Wildflowers, Designs for Appliqué and Quilting, Carol Armstrong

Willowood, Further Adventures in Buttonhole Stitch Appliqué, Jean Wells

Yvonne Porcella, Art & Inspirations, Yvonne Porcella

For more information write for a free catalog from:

C&T Publishing, Inc.
P.O. Box 1456
Lafayette, CA 94549
(800) 284-1114
http://www.ctpub.com
e-mail: ctinfo@ctpub.com